Bob Barner and YOU

Bob Barner and YOU

Bob Barner

The Author and YOU

Sharron McElmeel, Series Editor

LIBRARIES
UNLIMITED
A Member of the Greenwood Publishing Group

Westport, Connecticut · London

Library of Congress Cataloging-in-Publication Data

Barner, Bob.
  Bob Barner and you / Bob Barner.
    p. cm. — (The author and you)
  Includes bibliographical references and index.
  ISBN 1-59158-262-8 (pbk : alk. paper)
  1. Barner, Bob. 2. Authors, American—20th century—Biography.
3. Illustrators—United States—Biography. 4. Children's literature—
Authorship. 5. Picture books for children—Authorship. 6. Children's
literature—Illustrations. I. Title.
PS3552.A67377Z46 2006
813′.54—dc22   2006023644
[B]
British Library Cataloguing in Publication Data is available.

Library of Congress Catalog Card Number: 2006023644
ISBN: 1-59158-262-8

First published in 2006

Libraries Unlimited, 88 Post Road West, Westport, CT 06881
A Member of the Greenwood Publishing Group, Inc.
www.lu.com

Printed in the United States of America

♾™

The paper used in this book complies with the
Permanent Paper Standard issued by the National
Information Standards Organization (Z39.48–1984).

10 9 8 7 6 5 4 3 2 1

SPECIAL THANKS

I would like to thank all of these people who in the past
and present have taken a helpful interest in my career:
Catherine Barner, Al Beck, John and Kate Briggs, Al Capp,
Mary Cash, Doug Duchin, Martin Dunn, Libby Ford,
Sara Gillingham, Regina Griffin, Guy's Lunch crowd, Bob Hale,
Jack Jensen, Trina Schart Hyman, Morris Kirchoff, Mr. Krabill,
Valerie Lewis, James Marshall, Emilie McLeod, Mary Meehan,
Mom and Dad, Victoria Rock, Joan Stevenson, Liza Voges,
Andy Warhol, and Paul Szep.

Bob Barner

Contents

Series Foreword

Have you ever wanted to sit down and talk with the author of a beloved story? Have you ever wanted to find out more? Good authors are like good friends. They touch our hearts and minds. They make us wonder, and want to learn.

When young readers become engaged with story, they invariably ask questions.

- Why is Gerald McDermott so fascinated with myths and legends? How did he locate and choose which stories he wished to retell? Are the images in his books faithful to the culture they represent?
- Did Alma Flor Ada know the people that we meet in her stories? Why does she write in Spanish and English?
- Can Toni Buzzeo tell us how much of *The Sea Chest* is legend and what part is fact? What character does she like best: the Dawdle Ducking, Papa Loon? How does she get her ideas?
- How long does it take Jim Aylesworth to write and retell his stories? Did he always know that he wanted to be a writer and poet?
- How does Jacqueline Briggs Martin find the inspiration for her stories? How does she research the facts for her stories?

As teachers and librarians, we know that the moment children begin asking questions; we are presented with a wonderful opportunity. In response, we may hold discussions or create learning activities. Yet, answers to some questions are hard to come by. After all, our students and we cannot just sit down and talk with the authors we love and admire. But, wouldn't it be great if we could?

Libraries Unlimited has developed *The Author and YOU* series to give you the next best thing to a real life visit with your favorite children's authors and illustrators. In these books, you'll hear from authors and illustrators as they reflect on their work and explain to YOU, the reader, what they really had in mind. You'll find answers to some of the questions you and your students might ask, and to some you never thought to ask.

Just as each author or illustrator is a unique individual, so will his or her conversation with YOU be unique and individual. There is no formula, no pre-designed structure. We've simply asked each author or illustrator to discuss the things they think are important or interesting about themselves and their books—and to share their comments with YOU.

Some authors will provide actual ideas and plans for you to use in sharing books with young readers. Others will share ideas that will help you generate your own ideas and connections to their work. In some cases the author writes the book in collaboration with another. In others, it is a private reflection; but in all cases you'll discover some fascinating information, and come away with valuable insights.

Previously this series has featured some notable authors and illustrators: Gerald McDermott, Alma Flor Ada, Toni Buzzeo, Jim Aylesworth, and Jacqueline Briggs Martin. This current addition to the series is authored by Bob Barner, an author and illustrator who creates his stories with words and pictures. Barner uses rhymes and rhythms to entice readers into his books—and then keeps readers coming back again and again to revel in the brilliantly executed illustrations. We are excited to present Bob Barner's perspective on his writing and art.

It is our hope that by giving you these special messages from authors and illustrators, *The Author and YOU* series will increase your joy and understanding of literature—and in turn, will help YOU motivate young readers, surround them with literacy and literacy activities, and share the joy of understanding.

Sharon Coatney
Sharron McElmeel

Biography

GROWING UP WITH ART

Art was always like a friend to me. As an only child there were many times when I was soothed, encouraged, entertained, and comforted when I was making art. Many of the members of my extended family have both artistic and musical talents. I had two uncles who could draw very well, and several people in the family are self-taught amateur musicians. The only other writer in the family was my maternal grandmother, Francis Koehller. She wrote the "what's new and who's visiting whom" column for the *Tuckerman Record* newspaper in Tuckerman, Arkansas, for many years in the 1950s and 1960s. She also played the pump organ at church on Sundays and at her home. I

My Parents and Me

1

always looked forward to visiting her for a few days in the summer and playing the antique pump organ.

Most of the picture books I had when I was growing up were Little Golden Books—not books from the library, but rather from the supermarket. They were sold in wire racks at the end of the cereal aisle. My mother would bribe me by saying that she would let me choose a book if I behaved while we did the shopping. During our shopping trips I chose *The Three Little Pigs, Jack and the Beanstalk*, many books beautifully illustrated by the wonderful illustrator Gustaf Tenggren, and lots of nonfiction books, my favorites. Dinosaurs, sharks, farm animals, dogs, cars, classic fairy tales, and outer space were popular themes. My taste for nonfiction began at an early age.

When I wasn't reading or drawing, I was involved in normal childhood activities.

Although I loved drawing, I don't think I excelled as an artist in my first years at elementary school. I had to go through the process of overcoming my intimidation by materials and discovering my personal abilities. I went through all of the phases young artists seem to pass through—conquering a new technique, learning to draw realistically, applying color, and making a good design or composition. When I was in the third grade, another interest blossomed. I started playing the acoustic guitar—or trying to play—when I was

about eight years old. My father always played the guitar at home on the weekends or in the evenings. When my hands finally got big enough to fit the fingerboard I started plucking out a few simple tunes myself. I became obsessed with guitar music and practiced whenever I wasn't studying, drawing, or outside playing sports. I also watched all of the guitarists I could find on the television shows to see how the professionals played their music. I remember looking through the *TV Guide* on Sundays and marking the performers I wanted to see during the next week.

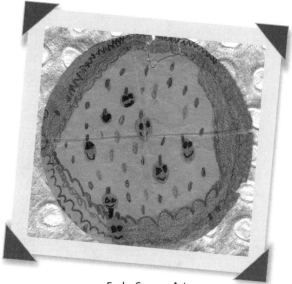

Early Crayon Art

I saw Chuck Berry on the Steve Allen Show and Andres Segovia on Ed Sullivan. It was a lot of fun. We had a piano and a violin in the house that I spent some time with, but the guitar was my instrument of choice. My appreciation of art and music was in full bloom by the time I was eight years old. I practiced the guitar on my own at home, but I continued to take as many art courses as I could at school.

I finally began to enjoy drawing even more in high school, when I had lots of fun drawing just about anything in a realistic manner as the result of all of my practice. During those years I felt a sense of satisfaction every time I finished a still life or portrait that looked just like the model. I spent most of my time that wasn't taken up with school or sports practicing the guitar or working on art projects. Then another door opened when a new art teacher arrived at school.

TWO GREAT TEACHERS

I was very fortunate to have two great art teachers early in my life: my sixth grade art teacher, Mr. Krabill, and my high school art teacher

Teacher's COMMENTS

WILLOUGHBY-EASTLAKE CITY SCHOOLS

PERIOD 4

We have enjoyed Bobby's Art work and his hobbies. He is a good student and I enjoyed having him.

ASSIGNMENT FOR THE YEAR 19 56 19 57 GRADE 3

PROGRESS IN HABITS

The home and the school share a great common purpose—the growth and progress of children. The school makes a serious effort to promote your child's physical, emotional, mental and social development. Following is our rating of certain important social and work habits:

SOCIAL HABITS	REPORT PERIOD I	II
Works and plays well with others	B	A
Respects the rules of the school	B	A
Offers good ideas	B	A

WORK HABITS		
Works well by himself	B	A
Completes work on time	B	A
Works in a neat and orderly manner	B	A
Follows directions	B	A
Takes care of materials	B	A
Takes care of wraps	B	A

ATTENDANCE RECORD

Only your child's illness, or other unusual causes, should prevent prompt and regular attendance.

Days Absent	7	7
Times Tardy	0	0

EXPLANATION OF MARKS
A Excellent C Fair F Failing
B Good D Weak

PROGRESS IN SKILLS

Kindergarten experiences form the basis for much of your child's progress and success, and help to develop a readiness for reading and arithmetic.

	REPORT PERIOD I	II
Readiness for Reading	B	A
Includes good listening, recall of stories and experiences, and clear speech.		
Readiness for Arithmetic	B	A
Includes an understanding of numbers in games and other class activities.		

10-22-53

FIRST REPORT PERIOD TEACHER'S COMMENTS

a very satisfactory pupil, he does especially well in drawing.

PARENT'S COMMENTS

for all three years, Mr. Al Beck. Mr. Krabill visited my sixth grade classroom twice weekly at H. W. Longfellow Elementary School. He would knock on the door and push his art cart into the room. The cart was filled with wonderful new materials every week. During his art classes I had my first experience with pottery-making, using glazes, oil painting, sculpture, and the study of color concept. He seemed to take an interest in all of his students, and especially the ones like me who caught his enthusiasm for the creative projects he prepared for us. I remember the excitement in the room when our first finished glazed ceramic pieces were returned from a commercial kiln outside the school. While making our first pottery pieces, we had learned something about construction, engineering, mathematics, color sense, design, and, most importantly, meeting a deadline with our clay project. I remember being excited and nervous at the same time when he told us that if our ceramics weren't properly prepared they would likely explode when fired in the kiln at 1,000 degrees. This would destroy not only the poorly made sculpture but many of those around it. Such pressure! I had worked for weeks on a large ceramic likeness of Frankenstein. I think it was probably very ugly. But I was given a nice pat on the back for my efforts by Mr. Krabill.

June 13, 1960
Longfellow School

Dear Mr. and Mrs. Barner,

This past year, I have had the opportunity of watching and guiding an <u>unusual</u> art talent, namely your son, Robert.

Sincerely,
Carl R. Krabill
Art Instructor

Mr. Krabill had a gift for creating projects that were of particular interest to his young students. The subject of this sculpture was my own choice. I remember thinking it was a terrific idea at the time. At the end of the school year he gave me a letter to take to my parents. The letter acknowledged my talent, but its purpose was to encourage my parents to support me in my artistic interests. This was a very insightful and generous thing to do. I didn't realize it at the time, but after the letter arrived my parents became more tolerant of my large art projects spread out on the kitchen table and lurking in the garage. His letter was a wonderful gift.

Al Beck was quite unique in Eastlake, Ohio. He was not only head of the art department at North High, he was also a working artist who had done postgraduate study at the Sorbonne. I think he was the first "real" artist I ever met. I was very fortunate to be exposed to Mr. Beck during my three years at North High, at a time when I was beginning to open my eyes to a larger picture of the art world. He led some of the most spirited and creative classes of my education, in high school or in college. Mr. Beck had unique and fascinating ways of introducing each new area of study. One of his early presentations involved asking his class how many views we could draw of the Mason jar he was holding in his hand. After some discussion, the class confidently agreed that the jar could be drawn from six angles: the top, bottom, and four sides. Mr. Beck began to count as he very slowly turned the jar until he finally reached the number 100. Then he dropped the jar. It broke into hundreds of pieces with a deafening crash. Listening to him count to one hundred had a soporific effect on all of the students in the class, by design. We were all startled and amazed with his demonstration. This is a moment I'll never forget. He then moved to a slightly different angle and continued to count the hundreds of shards on the floor. When he reached about 120, he looked up and said, "You get the idea." When I heard the glass shatter on the floor of the art lab, I immediately got it. It was the beginning of my thinking in a different way about art. This was one of the early moments when I believe I began to think outside the box and began to get in touch with my own creativity.

Mr. Beck helped me prepare a portfolio of my best work to use as a part of my college admission process. During the course of my senior year, he stayed late one night per week to help me create, select, and present a portfolio that would eventually help get me a scholarship to art school. Creating my first portfolio was quite an incredible challenge. Mr. Beck had a technique in which I would put all of what I considered my best work on a chalk ledge. After stepping back a few feet, we would both scrutinize every piece. It became obvious when seeing all of the pieces as a group that some of the work was not exceptional. These pieces were either removed from consideration or improved with more work and considered for possible inclusion again. This process forced me to become more critical of my own work and, most importantly, helped me begin to develop a critical artist's eye.

Mr. Beck also organized a senior class trip to New York City for his art class. We were booked into the Empire Hotel for three nights. For most of us, it was the first time seeing the Big Apple. We saw great museums, shops—including a trip to Georg Jensen to see firsthand what first-rate design looked like—Greenwich Village, and *The Fantasticks*, an off-Broadway play. This was an inspiring few days I'll never forget. At one

Off to Art School

point we were given about an hour of free time to roam around and explore the area of the East Sixties. It was filled with galleries, shops, and restaurants that cooked exotic foods like nothing I had ever smelled in Eastlake, Ohio. I walked into a tiny jewelry shop that caught my eye; actually, I think I was buzzed in. I was looking at the jewelry in the cases that was obviously handmade with gold and precious stones when I became aware of a very pale man with a shock of gray hair and glasses. I couldn't believe I was standing next to Andy Warhol. I couldn't believe he was actually buying something. The prices seemed astounding to a kid who worked in a drugstore on the weekends. I mentioned what had happened to a few of the other kids, but I don't think anyone believed me. But my brief meeting with Andy Warhol was the cherry on top of my first trip to the Big Apple. My father recently reminded me that the cost for the trip was a whopping $73, not including meals. Those were the days.

EDUCATION

I graduated from Columbus College of Art and Design in 1970 with a B.F.A. degree in illustration and a minor in advertising and art history. I grew up in Northern Ohio. Going to school in Columbus was just far enough from home that I felt independent but close enough that I could still get back for a weekend once in a while. I had several influential teachers at CCAD, but none was more important than the dean of the school himself. Dean Canzanni taught a course called color concept. This class was important to me because I felt that drawing and design were my strengths but that I needed a better understanding of how to use color effectively. The class was a rigorous introduction to color theory and was taught in a theatre setting. Every week after the lecture, we were given an assignment using a concept about color. I found these assignments to be quite challenging but a great learning experience. I began my career at school as a fine art major and later switched to advertising and illustration with a minor in art history. During the first year I took the foundation year courses, followed by three years of elective classes. I chose a mix of academic, studio arts and what I felt were practical application classes.

I knew I wanted to work in the field of art after graduation. Advertising was a very exciting field in the 1960s. There were lots of groundbreaking ad campaigns on TV and especially in print. The use of photography and illustration was flourishing. Printing techniques were improving exponentially so that more and more images could be faithfully reproduced. Peter Max was one of the artists I admired at the time. To me he seemed to bridge the gap between illustration and fine art. I had kept a large collection of posters and magazine tear sheets of the work of my favorite illustrators during my last years in high school. I felt that my future would be in advertising, illustration, or possibly teaching. And that turned out to be the case. Upon graduation I wanted to move to New York, Los Angeles, or Boston to start my career. The creative centers were more isolated to the East or West Coasts in those days, and the possibilities for a career in the arts in Columbus seemed rather limited to me at that time.

WRITING THE FIRST BOOKS

I became interested in primary education and children's literature during my second year at CCAD. The school didn't offer a course in children's book writing or illustration. At the time the children's book market was very small, and developing a curriculum for students interested in children's literature just wasn't part of the plan of most institutions. While I was studying at school I made it my goal to learn as much as I could about children's trade book publishing. I visited the public library and became familiar with all of the classics, as well as the new books in the collection. I attended lectures when visiting authors were in town and read any children's literature how-to books I could find. While I was pursuing my own independent course of study, I started to develop some original ideas for books. Three years after graduating from school I finally did move to Boston. Within a week a friend of a friend introduced me to James Marshall at a dinner party in historic Marblehead.

James Marshall is the author and illustrator of the very popular *George and Martha* series, as well as many other books. I had lunch with Jim in Charlestown, near his home, the next week. Jim was not only the author and illustrator of the popular *George and Martha* books, he was also charming, witty, and very generous with his time and encouragement. Jim always seemed to be at the Ritz Carlton Hotel for breakfast or lunch. He led what seemed to me a very cosmopolitan existence and still managed to create many fantastic books. After Jim's encouragement, I was even more determined to have a book published.

When I arrived in Boston I was driven to succeed. My dream was to create my own books, but I was also very interested in freelance illustration work. Illustration was a lucrative field at that time. On my second day in Boston I visited several advertising agencies and publishing companies with a portfolio of my best work. Within a few days I had landed my first job drawing the cover for the *Boston Phoenix*, a wildly popular newspaper tabloid that was sold mostly to college students all over the city. It was quite exciting to see my art on the cover of the *Phoenix* being hawked on all four corners of the major intersections in Boston. Not bad for only one week in a new town. As the result of promotional mailings and calls to art directors to show my portfolio, I became very busy with illustration work within weeks of my move. My first break in the book world came when an art director with whom I interviewed at *The Atlantic* magazine suggested that the work in my portfolio was well suited for children's books. The art director asked if I had some time that afternoon and made a call to her colleague a few blocks away. I was asked to come to the editor's office across the Boston Common right away. Thirty minutes later I was showing my work to Emilie McLeod, senior editor at Atlantic, Little Brown Publishing. Emilie was a lovely, intelligent, and wise person. She was also the editor for some very talented young author/illustrators. David McPhail, *The Bear's Toothache*, and Marc Brown, the creator of the *Arthur* series, were both making books with Emilie. The books she edited were beautiful and rather exquisite, especially considering the technical limitations of the time. Most of the books were printed with only a few colors because at the time full-color printing was incredibly expensive. At the end of our time together she said she liked my work very much and that if I ever had an idea for one of my own books to let her know about it. I played it cool as I thanked her for her time and left the office. However, I can't remember walking home, I was so excited.

FIRST SUBMISSIONS

I started submitting book ideas to publishers while I was still in art school. Most of my manuscripts were returned with rejection letters filled with excellent tips for making the work better.

I wish I still had them. It was a kinder, gentler time, for sure. I like to think that the editors who took the time to look over my ideas saw at least the seed of a unique idea in them. I was always disappointed

when my proposals were returned. But I knew that with each submission I learned something that put me closer to my goal of being published.

GETTING PUBLISHED

> **THE ELEPHANT'S VISIT**
> *Bob Barner, illustrated by the author.* Little, Brown (Atlantic)
>
> The author-illustrator hits the jackpot with his first book, a wordless wonder which little ones can handle on their own. A series of bright, big pictures shows the plight of a strange little creature whose friend, an elephant, comes to visit. The huge beast makes the bull in a china shop seem delicate. Elephant tries to be a thoughtful guest but he breaks chairs, the bed and even doorways in the house of his host. The two go for a short boat ride and the boat sinks. In short, the suffering friend is relieved when the elephant's mother arrives to take her child home. (5–8)

When I got home from that first meeting with Emilie McLeod, I pulled my favorite book idea out of the top drawer of a chest in my bedroom/studio. I had come up with an idea for a book about elephants some time before. I made a few changes to the dummy and waited about two weeks before calling Emilie to say that I had something to show her. We had a good meeting. She seemed enthusiastic about the concept and said she would present it to the children's book board at the next meeting. I'm not sure I really understood what this meant at the time, but I knew it was good news. Most editors can't choose to publish a book without presenting it to the board. Decisions are made about which book proposals to publish by the board in publishing companies. The board is usually made up of various editors, as well as people involved in the financial and marketing aspects of the company. Fortunately, I was very busy with other

illustration and design projects while I waited for an answer about my book idea from Emilie.

I was at my parents' house in Ohio for Christmas vacation when the phone rang on Christmas Eve. My father answered the phone, turned to me, and said, "It's for you." It was Emilie calling from Boston with wonderful news. Little, Brown was going to publish my book. After all of my work and study to get published, that was one of the best Christmas presents I've ever had. I seemed to be floating on air through the entire Christmas holiday. Emilie was incredibly kind to call me during the holidays as soon as the decision about my book was made. I'm sure she knew it would mean a lot to me. And she was right. Within a week I had signed a contract for *The Elephant's Visit*. The story would be told entirely with pictures. No text at all. I was encouraged to try this approach after the editor looked over my

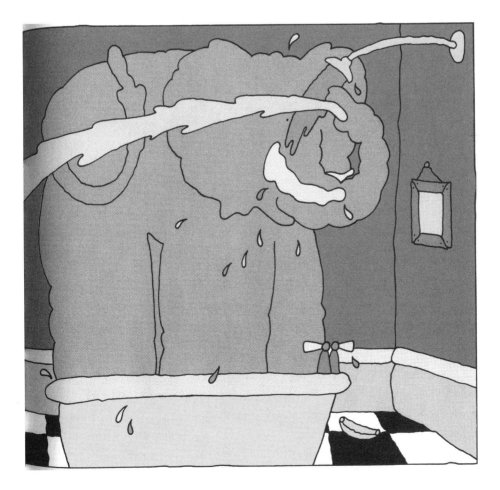

detailed drawings. She was right. The pictures really did tell the story. Because full-color printing was very expensive in 1975, I had to prepare an overlay for each of the spreads. The art style I used was almost cartoon like. I drew a thick black outline for each of the objects or characters on the pages. Then I used an amberlith film cut with an X-Acto knife to make camera-ready color separations for each spread. Amberlith is an amber-colored film adhered to a clear thin plastic sheet. The shapes that will be used to identify areas of color are defined by using a sharp X-Acto blade to cut and peel away portions of the amber film. This was very tedious and time consuming and not an exact science. Today's art is created as reflective art. You make the art you want and prepare it for printing with a digital camera, scanner, and computer. The result on the printed page can look very much like the original art.

The next book I wrote and illustrated myself was *Elephant Facts* (Dutton, New York, 1979). I don't really know what the fascination with elephants is all about. This was my first nonfiction book of facts. Emilie McLeod actually suggested the idea. "Let's try a book of facts," she said. I guess we had elephants on our minds because of the earlier book. Emilie's idea was to do this book in an even more comic book-like technique. She felt strongly that the format would appeal to readers who were spending a lot of time and money on comic books at the time. Believe it or not, I had to create the art in the same way I did for *The Elephant's Visit.* All of the art was pre-separated, with overlays cut with X-Acto blades. It was still just as tedious four years later. Thank goodness for computers and modern printing techniques that allow me to simply create my collage art and give it to the art director and book designers.

SUNDAY FUNNIES

Shortly after I finished *The Elephant's Visit,* I got a call from someone claiming to be Al Capp. Al Capp was the famous creator of the
popular *Li'l Abner* comic strip. He knew all about my new book and
asked me if I would like to come to his studio to audition for a job
as his assistant. This was all sort of weird because the book wasn't
being published for months. Only the people at Little, Brown Publishing knew about the book at that point. Besides, I always thought that
Al Capp worked out of New York. I asked a few questions to verify
that it was Mr. Capp and felt somewhat satisfied that it was. We
agreed on a time the next day for me to come by and "audition," as
he called it. The next day was Sunday—a weird day for a job interview. I was quite suspicious of the circumstances for the interview and

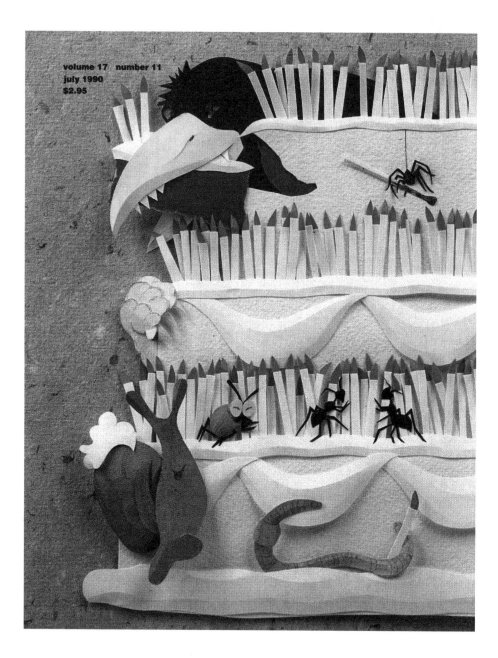

volume 17 number 11
july 1990
$2.95

almost cancelled the appointment. I walked to the address on Beacon Street in Boston. It was less than fifteen minutes from my house. I pressed the button that said "Capp." I was buzzed into the building and took the elevator to the top floor.

Then it happened. The elevator doors opened directly onto the apartment. I was looking at a very large foyer covered with *Li'l Abner* wallpaper. If this was a joke, it was an elaborate one. The next sound

I heard was a clip clop, clip clop coming down the hall. I knew that Mr. Capp had lost a leg as a child. Then from around the corner appeared Al Capp. I couldn't believe it was really him. Trademark red suspenders and all. I was really ready for a pie in the face from a friend. I thought the circumstance was too weird, and I had convinced myself that I was being set up by some of my practical joker friends. Mr. Capp invited me in and said that he liked my *Elephant*

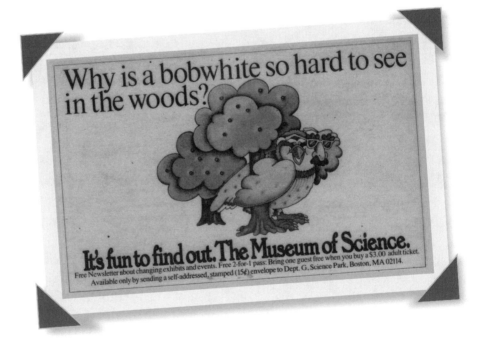

book. I asked how he knew about it and he said that the receptionist at Little, Brown, a family friend, had told him about me. It turns out that he had been searching far and wide for a replacement for one of his longtime assistants who had retired to California. Al had interviewed or auditioned artists from all over the country, including some from *Mad Magazine.* He told me he was looking for someone to do lettering and the talk balloons that surround them as well as some of the pencil work for the figures. Then the official audition began. I was seated at a rickety old drawing table, handed a beat-up pencil two inches long, and asked to draw a likeness of Daisy Mae using one of the cartoon strips as a guide. It seems that even as a kid I could always copy almost anything. So, I spent about ten minutes drawing what I thought was a decent likeness of Daisy Mae. Then came the moment of truth. Mr. Capp took a look at my drawing and said, "Looks great, kid. You're hired."

It was a wonderful feeling to be appreciated by a famous cartoonist whom I had grown up admiring. The funny thing was that I was just minding my own business and really wasn't looking for a job. My career was starting to take off. I had already quit my advertising job to concentrate on my personal work and publishing. However, we agreed that I would start the following Monday and work two days per week. I spent the next few months doing lettering and drawings for the strip. Al liked to run all of his ideas past everyone in the office. I found it rather intimidating when on my first day the famous cartoonist asked me for an idea for the next strip. I enjoyed my time as an apprentice cartoonist, but after a few months I was anxious to get on with my own projects and decided to leave the cartoon world of *Li'l Abner* forever.

ILLUSTRATION AND DESIGN

For the next few years I worked as an illustrator and designer in Boston. I did freelance work for all of the advertising agencies, the major textbook publishers, newspapers, magazines, and museums while maintaining my passion for making books. I also had a job as an art director, designing advertisements for one of the large agencies in Boston. The design managers quickly saw my flair for creating whimsical kid-friendly ads for institutions like the New England Aquarium and the Museum of Science in Boston. Around 1976, Trina Schart Hyman contacted me to do a project for the then-new *Cricket Magazine*. I was delighted to be associated with this great children's magazine and was thrilled to be called by a fine illustrator and art director like Trina. She earned the Caldecott Medal in 1985 for her illustration of *Saint George and the Dragon*. Trina hired me many times to do illustrations for *Cricket* over the next few years. She would always send a hand-written note when my project was completed to thank me for the art I had contributed to the magazine. These notes meant a lot to me, and I try to remember to do the same when I want someone to know that he or she is appreciated. Every time I worked for *Cricket* I was usually assigned nonfiction projects, which seemed to be becoming my specialty. When I worked for *Cricket* I felt as if I was a part of the children's book world. I had some other wonderful clients when I was in Boston as well, including the New England Aquarium and the Museum of Science. I enjoyed doing illustration projects for both places, but in many cases I was

With Bo and Luddie on Cape Cod

asked to design and illustrate the projects. I was usually hired for these jobs because the clients liked the books I made and wanted their project to have a similar character. I created a lot of non-fiction graphics, booklets, posters, and newsletters for both institutions. I worked for all of the advertising agencies in Boston and New York and continued to get

My wife, Cathie, and me at the Bologna International Children's Book Festival

illustration assignments from my art agent, Libby Ford, at Kirchoff/Wohlberg Inc. in New York.

Most of the Kirchoff/Wohlberg projects were for the large educational publishers like Houghton Mifflin, Harcourt Brace, or McGraw Hill. I usually enjoyed doing projects for these companies. After all, the work was nonfiction, my favorite. My wife, Cathie, and I continued to live in Boston until 1996, when we moved to San Francisco. We were both interested in moving to a city with a larger creative community. San Francisco has been a wonderful new beginning for both of us. And many of our friends here are real artists! I look forward to the next West Coast chapter of our lives.

My Creative Process

KEEPING AN IDEA FILE

I make notes or sketches for all of my new book ideas. Some of the ideas start as simple doodles or the book title or simply the identification of a topic I find interesting. I get my ideas by asking myself what I am truly interested in. If I have a passion for a subject, I know there's a chance it may make a good book. Young readers and their teachers that I meet at school visits also suggest ideas they would like to see made into books. I put all of these ideas in a small notebook. That way I don't lose or forget them, and I know where they are when I have time to work on the ideas. I choose to use a notebook so I can sketch, write, or tape photo references onto the pages.

Sketches from 1976 Bermuda notebook

RESEARCH

I love to do research for my books. Most of my work is nonfiction so I do need to visit my local library to check out the details. I have also found the Internet a great place to check facts.

When I can, I like to find an expert on the subject I'm writing about. A real live scientist may have the latest information on the subject of his or her special field. I use as many photo references as possible when I am refining my sketches. I can usually, but not always, draw almost anything on first try. My ability to draw well is the result of practice and all the drawing courses taught by very talented teachers that I took during my four years at art school. I seem to be able to catch the essence of most animals or objects. Using references helps me add the details that make the subject of the drawing unique. When I was making *Bugs! Bugs! Bugs!* I needed a photograph for the ladybugs. At the very time I was thinking about finding a photo, a ladybug flew in through the window and landed on my wrist. The ladybug stood quietly for a moment and then slowly turned around in a 360-degree circle, displaying all of the body parts. This was just the information I needed, and it saved me a trip to the library or an Internet search.

COLLAGE

Many of the pieces of art we admire in our great museums were created with collage artwork. Henri Matisse, Paul Klee, and Pablo Picasso all worked in collage during their careers. I have always liked working with collage, but I feel especially drawn to it when I am illustrating a book. *Benny's Pennies* was the first book that I illustrated completely with cut paper. With *Dem Bones,* I did my first true collage book. Working with children with collage art can be especially rewarding. The students don't seem to be as intimidated with the technique as they can be with paints or other media. From a practical standpoint, the cleanup is usually a bit easier as well. All you really need for a great collage workshop with a classroom is lots of colorful paper and glue sticks. Scissors can be optional. I have run a few workshops on Saturday mornings with twenty kids, and I'm happy to say that with just a little introduction from me they worked contentedly for a full two hours. Asking the students to bring in their own special collage materials for the projects gives them a feeling of investment in the class. They may collect things like used postage stamps, pieces of foil, dry macaroni, cotton pipe cleaners, or glitter.

I make most of the art in my books by tearing the papers with my fingers. I start the work for each book with a visit to the paper collection in my large flat file in my studio. I look through the samples and then make a trip to the art supply store to add just the right colors to the stack. I also use papers that I make myself as well as bits and pieces of wrapping papers, bits of decorated shopping bags, buttons, feathers, beads, and fabric swatches. Almost anything can be used in a collage. I do the work for all of my books at same size. This helps me see exactly what the art will look like when it is reproduced. Some artists like to make the original art much larger than the final print size. Rarely, an artist will make the original work smaller than the final printed book. After I have done a pencil sketch for an illustration, I am ready to begin the finished artwork. I use the sketch like a pattern. I tape or staple the sketch to the paper I want to use for the collage. I cut or tear along the line of the sketch so I have the same shape as the sketch, but made out of the paper I have chosen. I usually start with the large background shapes as I build the collage. The last pieces I make will usually be the tiny detail pieces. So, I work from large shapes in the back to smaller shapes in the front. I don't glue any of the pieces down until the entire illustration is done.

This way I can move things around and change my mind about colors and textures until I'm satisfied with everything. When I finish the pictures for a book, I send a large box of art off to the publisher. That's always a happy day. The collage art may be photographed or scanned directly into the computer so the designer can begin to design the book. I enjoy the collaboration with the designers of my books. They always do something fresh with the type and layout that makes the book even stronger.

WHICH CAME FIRST—PICTURES OR WORDS?

Most of my books actually start with the text. This is a surprise to some people who assume that an artist would probably find inspiration in sketches or photo reference. My notebooks are full of sketches as well as written ideas, but I usually add the drawings after I've taken a first pass at the writing. The editor for my first book, Emilie McLeod, made a lasting impression on me when she told me that the only thing that matters is the finished book. She encouraged me not to get wrapped up in the art too early in the creative process. First make the idea great and worry about the execution of the art later. As a result of her coaching, I don't worry too much about the early sketches or the early punctuation of the text. It is most important to have a great idea that is original and something that I think will interest the kids and teachers and work in the marketplace. I try to have a current idea of the marketplace by talking to teachers and booksellers, and most importantly by listening to children.

EDITING THE TEXT

I love to edit the text for a book that I'm excited about. I know this sounds strange coming from an artist, but it has become one of my favorite tasks in bookmaking. When I have finished my first pass at the text, usually in longhand, I enter it into the computer. I like to print out a hard copy of the story and work on the changes with a pen. One of my favorite places to write is while I'm traveling on an airplane or a train. I don't ride trains very much these days, but I always enjoyed seeing my editor in New York and sketching or making notes on the train trip back to Boston. I find that for me, writing while flying is a real pleasure. There are no interruptions or telephones at 40,000 feet. It's great to have a story or sketch to get involved with when faced with a bad movie and bumpy air. I change the words or complete lines or entire sections of the story. Sometimes I make small doodles or sketches in the page margins to figure out the best way to present the information.

CREATING THE SKETCHES

All of my sketches begin as tiny little drawings called thumbnails, actually about the size of a thumbnail. These are a great way to develop many ideas for the pages without spending a lot of time on details in the drawings. The thumbnails are large enough only to allow for the gesture or general direction and design of the page. This is an excellent way for me to work and explore many options for each spread in the book. I know there will be time for details later.

A sketch for *BUGS! BUGS! BUGS!*

REVISIONS

I always make several versions of every sketch. I want to explore the different possibilities for each approach. After I combine the best parts of each sketch, I make a final master sketch for each page of the book. I give these sketches to my editor, who reviews each one. The editor makes comments on each page layout. I hope that most of the sketches are approved on the first pass, but sometimes the editor has an idea about what should be shown in the art. I always look forward to the collaboration, and the comments I get will only help make the book the best it can be.

YOUR CREATIVE PROCESS

Getting an Idea

I've never met a young author or illustrator who didn't have great ideas for books. They always choose a subject they love, which, by the way, is the best way to keep your interest in the project until it is completed. It's a good idea to write down subjects that you think would make a great book. When you are trying to think of a topic for your book, simply ask yourself what kind of book you would love to find in the library or bookshop.

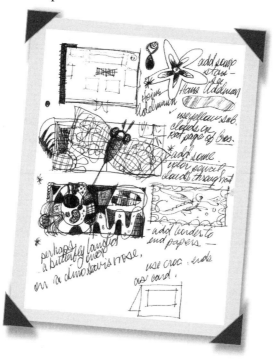

Creating the Art Style

Some of the artists who make books like to work in the same style for each project. However, some illustrators change their art technique for every project. When I start the sketches for a new book, I like to think of the best way to help bring the book to life. Most of my books are nonfiction, so I want to use art that will be clear and will present the information in the book in an accessible and visually interesting way.

Being Consistent with the Art Style

It can be difficult to illustrate an entire book in the same art style. Some adult illustrators, as well as many young artists, find their style changing as they work through the pages of a book. It's most important that the characters in a story remain recognizable throughout the book.

Books and Activities

SOME GENERAL HINTS FOR READING AND SHARING MY BOOKS

When sharing one of my books with students, it is best to follow these simple guidelines. Most of the books are composed of three parts: the art, the rhyming text or story, and the back matter information. In my experience with children, it is usually best to start out with the big picture. Literally show the book cover. Ask the class what the subject of the book is. Begin reading the text while holding the book so that everyone in the class can see. You may choose to do a second reading to share all of the facts written on the page or illustrated with the pictures. Finally, use the charts, diagrams, and other information in the back of the book to cover more specific and detailed information about the subject of the book. Some of the activities in this section are my own invention. But most of them are techniques I have seen during school visits all over the United States, as well as Guam and Mexico.

Credit, Anonymous

Credit, Anonymous

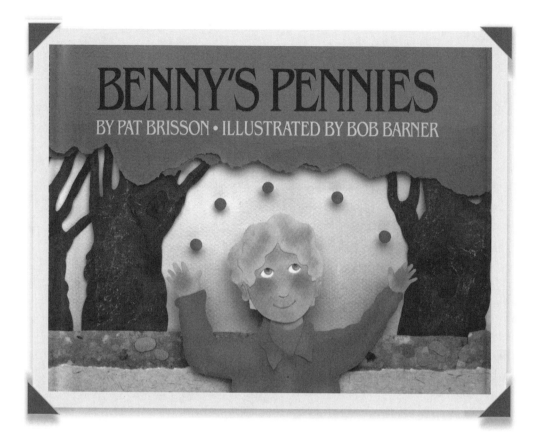

BENNY'S PENNIES

I loved the manuscript for *Benny's Pennies* the first time I read it. Pat Brisson wrote a wonderful story about a very generous little boy and all the things he bought with only five cents. My art agent, Libby Ford, at Kirchoff/Wohlberg in New York, was contacted by the editor of the book, Mary Cash, at Bantam Doubleday Dell in New York. Mary liked my work and asked if I would consider doing the art for the project. I was very happy to accept the job, but as I read the manuscript I began to have some ideas that I thought would make the art unique. I decided to make the illustrations as a series of dioramas. A diorama is defined as a miniature scene, wholly or partially three dimensional. I started with the background for each page of the book. The next layer or level of the art was suspended off the surface of the background with bits of paper or board attached to the back of my art. Clouds, trees, or some of the characters in the book came next. I continued to build the art until I added the final shape or shapes in the foreground. As the viewer sees the art, the section closest to the front is farthest from the background. After all of the original art was finished it had to be photographed for inclusion in the book. The printer scans the photographs into the computer. The photography process proved to be very difficult. The three-dimensional quality of the art created all sorts of shadows and unexpected color variations. The final photos that I was shown were actually the second set of shots. The editor was very nice to me and didn't let me know how difficult the process had been until all of their headaches were over. Had I known about the problems with the photos I would have been concerned about the whole project. The final result was fantastic. This was the first time the art in the book looked very much like the art I had created.

Something else made the art for *Benny* a little extra special for me as well. I had been to France and Italy for the first time just before I started working on the finished art for this book. I didn't really do much sketching on our trip. But when I got home and started sketching, many of the gnarly trees and landscapes that Benny walks by were inspired by the ancient weather-worn olive and cedar trees I saw on my trip. The result made for a book with a rather special look. Teachers like to use *Benny's Pennies* as a way to discuss sharing, money, and counting. As I drew the first sketches of Benny, the star of the story, I had a strong feeling that he should be about five years old with blonde hair and blue eyes. There were no physical attributes mentioned in the manuscript. I later found out that Pat's real-life son, Benjamin, was five years old and has blonde hair and blue eyes. She was quite shocked when she saw the printed book. It was a fun and unexpected connection.

A woman was cutting roses. Her name was Mrs. Hill.

Activities

One of my favorite reviews of this book said something like "Boy, this kid can really stretch a buck." Well, he did do well with his five pennies. Teachers have done some wonderfully creative things in using this little book as a way to teach kids about counting. I've seen several homemade board games that use a spinner to move Benny along the path until he must spend one more of his pennies. It's basically a race, but the players do have to make decisions about their five pennies along the way. *Benny* has also been packaged by third-party companies with the book, plastic pennies, and a tiny doll likeness of Benny and

"Will you sell me a rose?" asked Benny.
"Will you sell me a rose for a penny?"
"Yes, I will," said Mrs. Hill.

family. With these characters, even the very young kids can act out the story themselves.

When I present the book, I like to play a counting game. I read the start of the story so the audience knows that Benny has five pennies. Every time he buys another item for a penny, I ask how many he has left. The younger kids like to count down the loose change until no pennies are left. The confident counters lead the charge, while the more reluctant ones gain confidence as the number of pennies declines. At the end of the book I like to do a little review by asking what Benny bought for each member of his family—his dog, cat, brother, sister, and mother. After I draw the item I ask how many

A man was catching fish. His name was Mr. Beal.

pennies are left. By this time most of the students have great confidence in their answers. By the end of the presentation, the whole
group seems very comfortable with the concept of subtracting from
five. The book is also about sharing. Benny could have bought something for himself with his five bright and shiny pennies. He chose to
share his small fortune with his family instead. I love the fact that Pat
Brisson, the author, added another dimension to this story. It's a perfect message for a young person learning to count while being
reminded to share. I also talk about the art I made for the book, the
colorful collages I made with paper from all over the world. I had
never been to Europe until just before I started the art for this book.
Some of the gnarly trees that Benny walks by are styled after the ones

I saw during my travels. Finally, we discuss what other choices Benny could have made when he was shopping. It gives the students a chance to edit the story and be creative within the framework of the book.

DEM BONES

I grew up singing a song called "Dem Bones." "Dem Bones," sometimes called "Dry Bones," is a spiritual about resurrection that is used today as a song about the skeleton. If you sing "Dem Bones," you begin to understand how the skeleton fits together. It wasn't until many years later that I had the idea to use the 200-year-old spiritual as the basis of a picture book. One of the most enjoyable and inspiring experiences that I had while working on the book was listening to music. I found a few versions of the song and played them while I worked. I expanded my music library and found inspiration for the art at the same time. My literary agent, Liza Voges, suggested that we show my idea for the *Dem Bones* book to Victoria Rock at Chronicle Books in San Francisco. My wife and I were planning a vacation to the area, so I thought I would try to see her and present the project. I did arrange to see Victoria and show her a very early layout for the book idea. After viewing my material for a while, she said that to her this book was all about the art. Victoria probably never knew it, but her observation was extremely helpful in focusing the project in the right direction. I was

struggling with the balance of the book before her comment. Should it be dense with facts about bones and the song history or filled with magical illustrations balanced with the song and a few choice facts? The decision to allow my art to dominate helped this book become a reality. It is always useful when an editor can see the key to making a project work. The author can frequently be too close to the work to see the answer. That's exactly what Victoria did for me with her insight.

When I got back to my Boston studio, I did the first torn-paper collage prototype for *Dem Bones*. Victoria's comment sparked a great sample page and a wonderful book. There was one more obstacle in the way of making this book happen. I had read about the pending publication of another book by the same title. This situation is always crushing and happens much more frequently than you might imagine. Victoria wrote me a nice note suggesting that we wait and

NECK BONE

The neck bone is a continuation of the backbone or spine. It is made up of seven vertebrae called cervical vertebrae. These seven bones in your neck rotate so you can turn your head from side to side, nod yes or no and wiggle your head in time to music.

see what happened with the other book before we moved forward. Fortunately, when the book appeared it was a large pop-up paper-engineered presentation—a very different approach to book-making using the same song as inspiration. I see the different ways two artists interpreted the same information as rather interesting today, but it almost gave me a heart attack at the time. My friend Dr. Robert Wilkinson loaned me a few of his medical school books to search for bone facts and to bone up on the subject of the human skeleton. Dr. Wilkinson was a pediatric radiologist at Children's Hospital in Boston. He spent his days reviewing x-rays of children's bones.

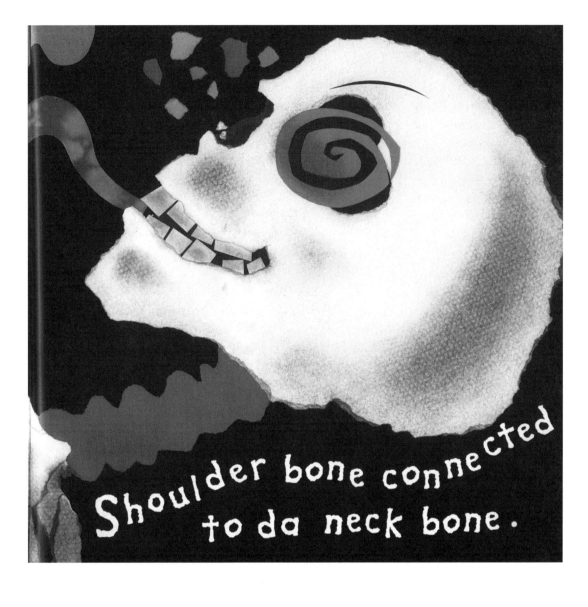

The perfect expert! He served as a wonderful scholar for the facts I used in the book. I dedicated *Dem Bones* to "My boney wife and to Dr. Robert Wilkinson, who is frequently humerus." I think they were both pleased.

One critical moment for the illustrations was when I decided to give the dancing skeletons a bit of a naughty edge. I wanted the skeletons to seem a bit mischievous, but not menacing. Maybe these were the skeletons of pirates after all. I had actually made two pieces of art. One was rather sweet and the other a bit edgy. I showed my wife the side-by-side comparison of the two pieces of art and asked her which one she thought best captured the spirit of what I was trying to do with the book. In other words, show a bunch of happy skeletons playing music and dancing around to a 200-year-old song. She chose the one I secretly preferred myself. Hooray! I work in such a vacuum that I look forward to the times when I can get the opinion of another person I respect. I always look forward to these little reality checks. I decided to go with the slightly edgy skeletons, and I'm glad I did. There's a fine line between fun art that's a bit naughty or silly and creating something that may worry or even scare the youngest readers.

I think my art is most successful when I work right up to the edge. All of the pieces of collage art for *Dem Bones* were torn out of paper. This is a very tedious and time-consuming task. The rather folk-art look that I obtained made it well worth the effort. Almost every book has a secret or special story. The cover you see on the front of *Dem Bones* is actually the second one I made. I tear or cut out all of the pieces for each piece of art I make. I don't glue anything down until every piece is made and put in place. This way I can move the bits and pieces around until I'm completely satisfied with the whole composition. Then, I can carefully lift up the edge of every piece of paper and glue it down. When I was making the cover art, it was a hot, rainy day in Boston. I had worked on the cover for two days and had many of the skeletons and their instruments completed and ready to glue down. I had cracked open a window before going to the other room to answer the phone. Just as I came back, I saw all the little bones rise up and get sucked out the window. Well, *Dem Bones* did rise up again, and then they flew out the window. I did get over it. Just not on the same day. So, unfortunately for me, that's why the cover for *Dem Bones* was made two times. Once with the window open. Once with the window closed.

It can be very difficult to choose the perfect type to complement the artwork in a book. The book designer, Cathleen O'Brien, had the brilliant idea to hire a calligrapher to create a typeface for the book. Lilly Lee, a very talented calligrapher, actually created a new font to embellish the words to the song that appear on every page of the story. This remains one of my favorite books to present. I love to play the song and draw along before the classroom as the different bones are mentioned. *Dem Bones* works well as a first body book for students. The book presents basic skeleton information in a unique and entertaining way. The art and music components just add to the fun. I am proud of the fact that many teachers open their unit on the body with my *Dem Bones* book.

Activities

This is one of my favorite books to present. I love to start a presentation with this book because I know everyone will have fun. There are several versions of the "Dem Bones" song available. I like to use the one from the *Rain Man* sound track. It is beautifully performed by the Delta Rhythm Boys. I like to briefly introduce the book and then start the music and draw along on a large pad as each of the bones is mentioned in the song. As the first bone, the toe bone, is sung, that's what I draw. I work my way up the skeleton and finish with the head bone as the song ends. Timing is everything. Drawing a stick figure along with the music is also very effective for teachers who would like to get their young anatomy students charged up. After drawing a large skeleton on the pad in front of the class, it's time for a group project. Play the song a few more time and ask the students to draw the skeleton along with the music. This little exercise has many benefits. It has yielded many wonderful skeleton drawings done in about two minutes. We all know young artists love to finish a project quickly and move on to the next. For some reason, there has been a spike upward in the number of Elvis skeletons that have been drawn for me lately. I don't get the connection, but the kids think it's hysterical. Talk about the collage skeletons in the book with the students. Much of the art was simply torn out of paper with my fingers. I think this gives the book a folk-art flavor that is perfect, in my opinion, since the idea was inspired by a 200-year-old song.

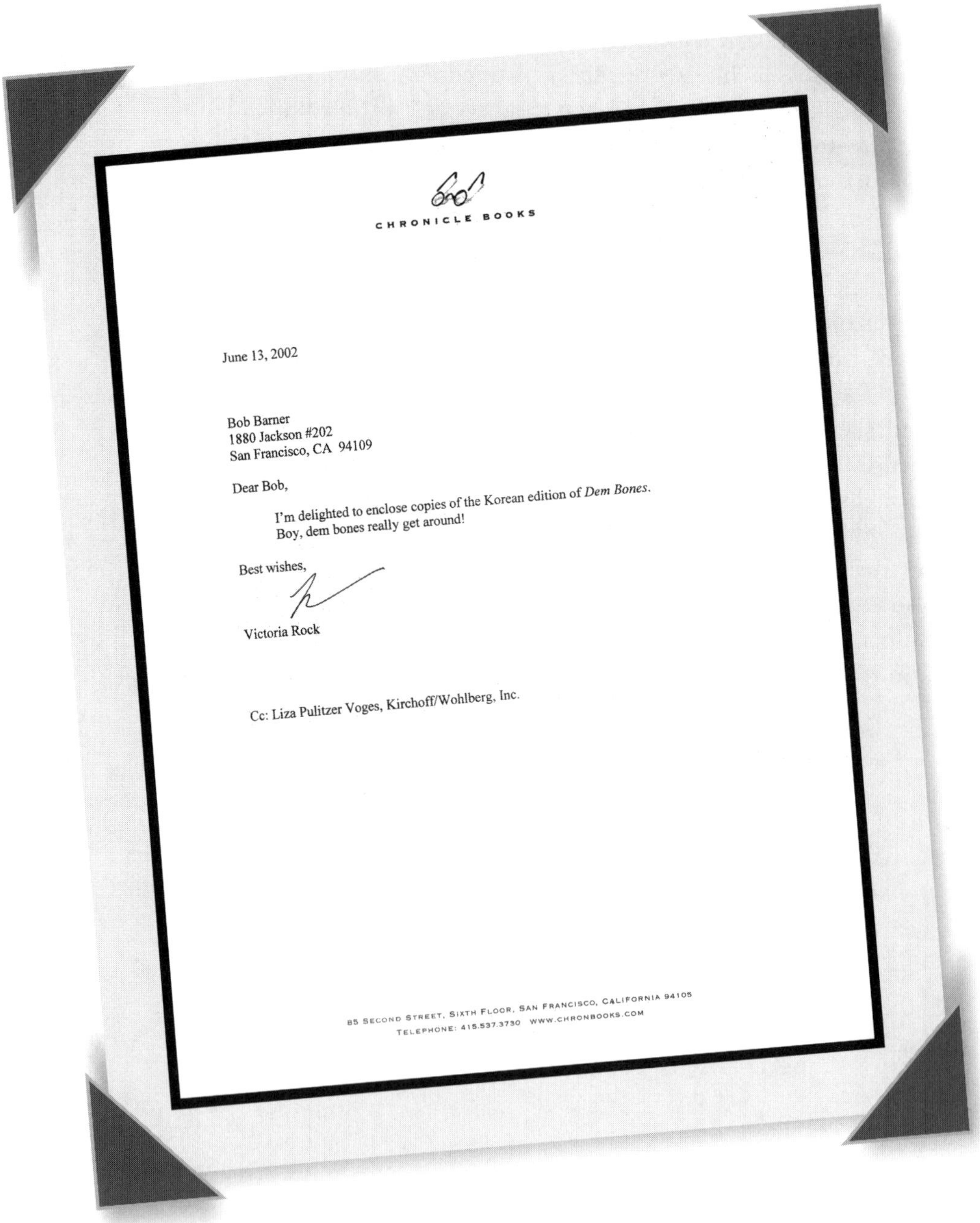

CHRONICLE BOOKS

June 13, 2002

Bob Barner
1880 Jackson #202
San Francisco, CA 94109

Dear Bob,

I'm delighted to enclose copies of the Korean edition of *Dem Bones*. Boy, dem bones really get around!

Best wishes,

Victoria Rock

Cc: Liza Pulitzer Voges, Kirchoff/Wohlberg, Inc.

85 Second Street, Sixth Floor, San Francisco, California 94105
Telephone: 415.537.3730 www.chronbooks.com

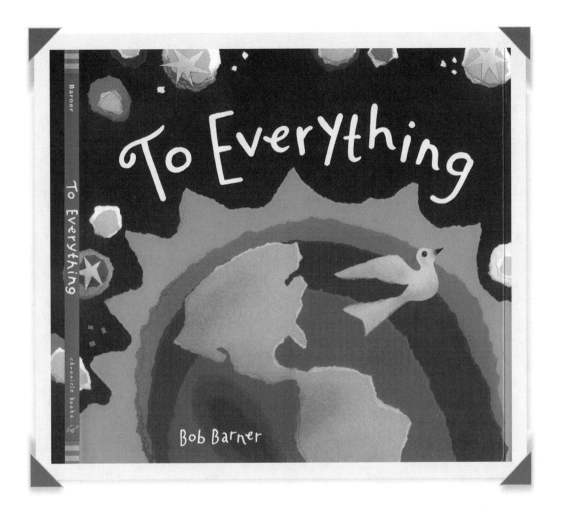

TO EVERYTHING

To Everything was my next book for Chronicle Books after *Dem Bones,* and the first Chronicle book I created while living in San Francisco. I was very excited about the project, especially after the success of *Dem Bones.* The idea for the book came from Ecclesiastes in the Old Testament. I have always loved the timeless passage that begins *"To everything there is a season and a time to every purpose under the heavens."* Pete Seeger has also written a beautiful song called "Turn, Turn,

After many sketches, I chose the image of a beautiful butterfly for my icon of the

Turn" based on the verse. I was listening to the song one day and simply saw the pages of a book turning as each line of the song was sung. I saw the project as a picture book that was a celebration of life and a forecaster of the future experiences students would have. I found it extremely difficult to strike a balance between an appropriate treatment of the text and creating kid-friendly images. I finally found the right path when I sketched the layout for the verse, a time to be born, a time to die.

celebration of life. This is still one of my favorite spreads I have ever done.

You never know what experiences publishing a book will bring to your life. *To Everything* has taken me on an interesting journey. One of the very first copies I signed was for a child who was just about to be born at a nearby hospital. That was the first time I had ever signed a book for someone who was not officially here yet. I have also been moved by the people who have asked me to sign a book in memory of a friend or loved one. *To Everything* may also be used as a tool for discussing emotions and as a springboard for understanding opposites

with very young readers. The author's notes and activities in the back of the book can be used to begin a class discussion about feelings, life cycles, conflict resolution, and giving and receiving. Several collage activities are suggested with each topic.

Activities

"Turn, Turn, Turn" is a beautiful song written by Pete Seeger. I like to play one of the many versions of the song and create a drawing as the music plays. After I introduce the book with the song and drawing, I read the book using the illustrations as a springboard to the text. Some of the couplets may seem a bit vague to young students. That's why I first talk about the illustrations and what's being depicted. With your students, read the book and show the illustrations. Read the author's note in the back of the book. *To Everything* captures love, hope, and joy, as well as the conflict that occurs in the course of life. The bright collages illustrate a simple verse that has a powerful meaning. *To Everything* can be used as a springboard for discussions about the choices we make and the effects of our actions upon others. These discussions may take place after a single reading of the book or over a period of time as different parts of the verse are explored.

As the book is read aloud, allow extra time for children to look closely at the illustrations. After a complete reading of the book, go back to the beginning and have discussions related to each spread. Ask the children to look at each page. Ask them if the images help them understand the meaning of the words more clearly. How? Invite the students to make their own collage with colored papers, magazine scraps, buttons, or used stamps. Give your collage a name and describe what it's about. *To Everything* demonstrates that changes are a part of life. "A time to plant, a time to pick" can be used as a springboard to a science discussion. *To Everything* can be used to discuss feelings, giving and receiving, cycles, and opposites. I have several binders full of beautiful little books of opposites created by classes I have visited and given to me as gifts. One first grade class got very literal and made some illustrations to accompany their text. The rhyme goes something like this: A time to stand up, a time to sit down. A time to be dry, a time to be wet. A time to be inside, a time to be outside. How refreshing and to the point. I have some real treasures from the kids that I will keep forever.

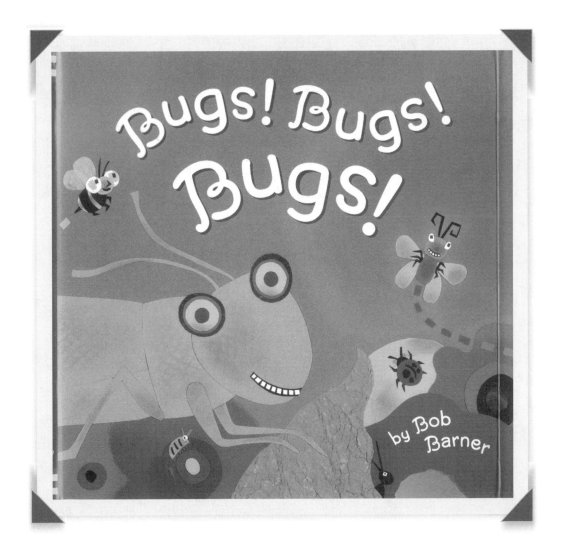

BUGS! BUGS! BUGS!

"Bugs! Bugs! Bugs! I want to see bugs" starts the first line of this book. I had the idea for this happy little insect tome after observing that very young children and early readers can have a very demanding way of asking for things at times. I loved the idea of a little entomologist who had an urgent need to see bugs, lots of bugs, and right now, please. The first title was *I Want to See Bugs*. That was later changed to *Bugs! Bugs! Bugs!* by my editor, Victoria Rock, as a way of making it obvious what the book is about. It's about bugs, by the way. I decided to come

up with a simple rhyming text and some bright non-threatening illustrations as a way to introduce young backyard explorers to the wonderful world of bugs. Since there are enough species to fill hundreds of volumes, I chose those most frequently encountered in yards and parks. I wanted some more information in the back of the book, so I enclosed an actual-size bug chart and I invented the Bug-O-Meter.

When I finish the art for a book, I put all of the illustrations in order against the studio wall. That way I can get a sense of the flow of

the art and how all of the images work together. I thought everything looked good, but I kept coming back to the spider page. I knew something just wasn't working, but I couldn't put my finger on it. I was looking at the colors, shapes, shading, and design. Finally I realized that I had been so preoccupied with the design elements of the art that I had given each of the spiders only six legs. How would I explain that one? Fortunately, my little ritual of looking everything over saved me great embarrassment.

Bug-O-Meter Chart

I have observed that the younger readers like to touch the pages with their fingers when they read. They like to trace the path of a flying bee in the illustrations or feel the tactile quality of the embossed bugs on the cover. I used this tactile appreciation to help create the Bug-O-Meter chart on the last spread. This picture book provides information with the art, the rhyming text, and the chart, which works best when a finger is used to connect the intersecting grids of facts. It provides information like how many legs each bug in the book has, or if it will sting or can fly. I like to play a game when reading this book to preschoolers and young readers. I

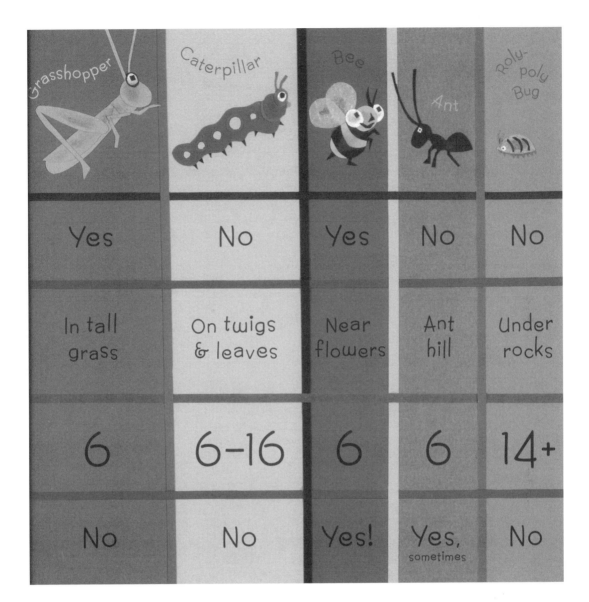

Grasshopper	Caterpillar	Bee	Ant	Roly-poly Bug
Yes	No	Yes	No	No
In tall grass	On twigs & leaves	Near flowers	Ant hill	Under rocks
6	6–16	6	6	14+
No	No	Yes!	Yes, sometimes	No

read the text and ask the audience to identify each new bug as I turn the page. This is a lot of fun for me and the kids, and I'm sure it is more engaging than simply watching me sit in a chair and read the story.

Activities

I like to ask the students to help me read this book. I think they feel empowered when they participate in the presentation. Hold the book up so it can be seen by everyone in the room. Ask the children to

ðð

CHRONICLE BOOKS

October 30, 2001

Bob Barner
1880 Jackson #202
San Francisco, CA 94109

Dear Bob,

I am delighted to be sending you the advances of the Korean edition of *Bugs! Bugs! Bugs!* I didn't know it was going to be so big! As far as books go, I love the smaller size of our edition. But this one is quite wonderful in that I feel as if I am holding the actual art in my hands. How amazing to have an art style that works at any size.
Congratulations!

Best wishes,

Victoria Rock

cc: Liza Voges/ Kirchoff & Wohlberg

85 SECOND STREET, SIXTH FLOOR, SAN FRANCISCO, CALIFORNIA 94105
TELEPHONE: 415.597.3730 WWW.CHRONBOOKS.COM

say the name of the bug they see as you turn each page. Read the text after they have said the name. Turn the page and wait for them to identify the next bug and read the text. Congratulate the bug identifiers for their sharp observations at the end of the story. Ask the children to look at the art and then ask them to find the bug that can sting. Ask them which bugs can fly and which bug has the most legs.

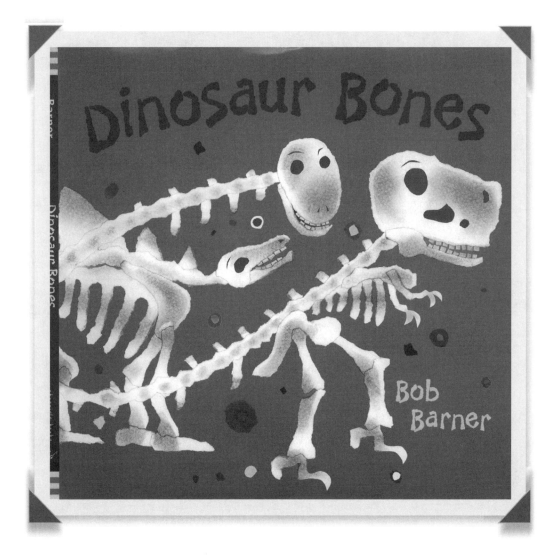

DINOSAUR BONES

I have always loved dinosaurs. It's hard to find a kid who doesn't, even sixty-five million years after they last walked the earth. Dinosaurs are just as popular today as they were when I was a boy.

I had the idea to use the same format as *Dem Bones,* but to talk about dinosaurs and dinosaur bones instead of the human skeleton. One thing I always do is check out the titles that already exist on the subject before I start my research. I usually do this by doing a search

on the Internet and checking out a local bookstore. I found a treasure trove of listings about dinosaurs. I was shocked to find the huge numbers of books on the subject. I knew I had to make my book unique if it was to succeed in the marketplace. I tried to do this by presenting dinosaur bones, scenes with dinosaur activities, a rhyming text, and dinosaur information in the back of the book. Like most of my books, this one is a bit of a hybrid. I have combined nonfiction facts with a rhyming fact-based text in a picture book format. To this I added colorful illustrations and a chart to give even more information.

I decided to take the approach that even though we only have dinosaur bones now, it is interesting to remember that they once walked the earth—and maybe right where you live. *"Dinosaurs are gone for good. Maybe they once lived in your neighborhood"* are the first lines of the book.

Dinosaurs had teeth to bite and jaws to chew.

The shape of the jaws and teeth help scientists find out if a dinosaur was a meat or plant eater. Dinosaurs with sharp teeth like this T. Rex were meat eaters.

Dinosaur Bones was very well received by the young paleontologists, and has been translated into French and Spanish, proving that the dinosaurs really do live on in spirit. I've asked myself why kids adore dinosaurs. I see a connection between dragons, giants, and other fantasy creatures. It seems fun for them to study something so gigantic, scary, and unique that has fortunately been extinct for the past 65 million years. When *Dinosaur Bones* was published, my wife and Chronicle Books gave me a wonderful dinosaur party, complete with a beautiful dinosaur cake. It was a nice way to launch the book and to celebrate its completion.

BOOKS AND BOB HALE

A starred review in Publishers Weekly means the book noted should be in every library and all alert booksellers will stock it. Bob Barner's latest, *Dinosaur Bones,* was reviewed on the first page of the July 9th Children's Books section with its title printed in red (not so favored titles are in black) and a big red star to draw the reader's attention. I seem to remember Barner's *Dem Bones,* a humorous take on the African spiritual, also received a starred review when it came out in 1996. *Dem Bones* received a Parent's Choice silver honor award and landed Bob on both the *Today Show* and *CBS Morning Show.* The former Duxbury resident's first job was drawing *Li'l Abner* for Al Capp. After a successful career in the commercial field, he turned to children's books and quickly made a name for himself with his unique artistry. He has

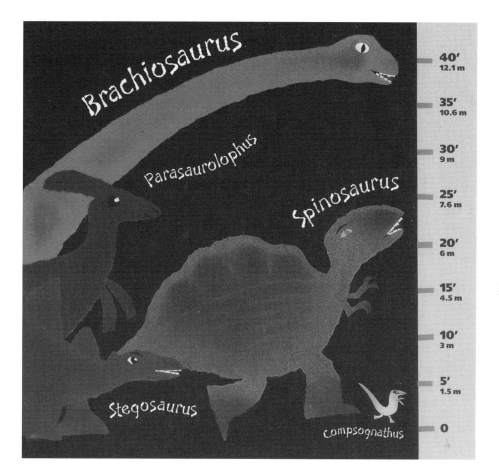

been published by Little Brown, Bantam, Doubleday, and Holiday House as well as Chronicle. My particular favorite of his earlier works is *Benny's Pennies*, which was a best-seller at Westwinds the year it was published. *Fish Wish* is a close second. Working with torn paper, collage, pen, ink, watercolor, and a computer, Bob Barner has created a signature style for his recent titles published by Chronicle Books of San Francisco: *To Everything* in '98, *Bugs! Bugs! Bugs!* And *Walk the Dog,* both in '99. To Everything, Bob's take on the words from Ecclesiastes, was nominated for a Golden Kite Award. *Bugs! Bugs! Bugs!* was an ABA Pick of the List.

Children and adults respond to the ever-present wit in his complex pictures, which always seem to hide something that will only be discovered the next time they are viewed. For Peaceable Kingdom Press, he produces bookmarks, story stickers, and a line of blank cards, which reflect this same humor. He has also become involved in doing artwork to promote events for the San

Francisco Bay Area Book Council. As if producing all this and doing books, for which he writes the text as well as creating the illustrations, isn't enough to keep one man busy, Barner has become a popular library and classroom speaker where he shows children how he makes characters using everything from fingerprints to Styrofoam. The latest book is the third he has done on the creatures that "... are gone for good. Maybe dinosaurs once lived in your neighborhood!" An elliptical verse drives the tale of *Dinosaur Bones*: "They had bones with disks and bones with points, bones for running with sockets and joints." Pictured are five dinosaur species, two that ate meat and three that ate plants. We see them as they looked walking the earth, and we see their skeletons. To augment the lines of verse, there are factual paragraphs on each page to instruct children who never seem to get enough on Stegosaurus, Triceratops, and their friends or enemies. The combination of whimsical and factual gives the book a reader interest range from two perhaps to eight. The final pages are a "dinometer" that has basic information on length, weight, etc., and what the animal's footprint looks like—in case we should come across such an indentation in our backyard. Bob Barner has batted another homer.

Bob Hale is a past president of the American Booksellers Association, a former bookshop owner, columnist, and novelist.

Activities

If you ever have trouble pronouncing the name of a dinosaur, just ask one of your students. I am always amazed that even the four-year-olds seem to know how to pronounce these complex words. Like compsognathus, for example. On the top half of a $9' \times 12'$ piece of art paper, let each of the students draw their favorite dinosaur. If any of them have trouble thinking of their favorite, which I doubt, ask them to look in the book for some ideas. After the art is completed, ask them to write a description of their dinosaur on the bottom half of the same sheet. They can include some nonfiction information like what or whom it ate, how much it weighed, how long it was, and when it lived. If they use one of the dinosaurs in my book, they can find this information in the back of the book. My experience has been that students will fill the page with numerous and accurate dinosaurs.

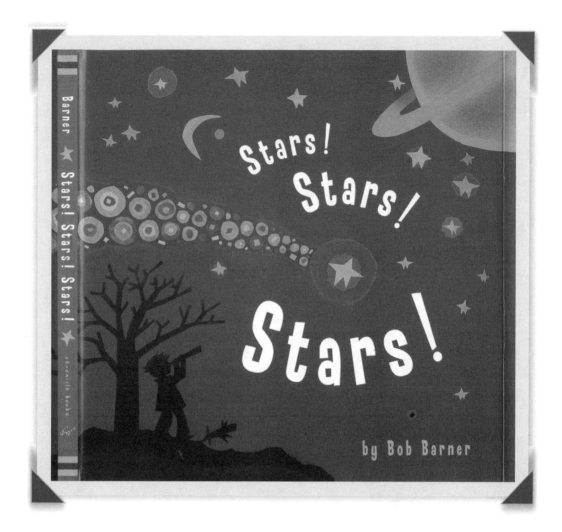

STARS! STARS! STARS!

I wanted to do another book similar to my *Bugs! Bugs! Bugs!* book. I thought about some of the other subjects that were of interest to me and are perennial favorites of children. Stars and planets seemed an obvious choice—obvious because I know teachers use the planets and stars as a part of their curriculum in kindergarten, and because it seems to me that every kid loves to find out about the stars, planets, and space. I knew the book would be useful in schools and would have a trade book appeal because of the interest in the subject. I did my research by using books on the subject, searching the Internet, and spending many inspiring nights gazing at the crystal-clear night skies above Sonoma, California. I did the art for this book in the summer of 2001. I always enjoy the

summers when I'm working on a book project. School is out, so there are no school visits. I enjoy the school visits very much, but it is also nice to focus on an entire book until it's completed. Summer was a perfect time to do the art for this book. I could see planets, stars, constellations, and shooting stars almost every evening if I needed to do a little research. I didn't want to simply write facts about stars but to actually evoke the excitement that a young stargazer shows when he or she observes the heavens. I started the rhyming text by talking about stars and planets to broaden the subject of the book. I wrote about all of the planets, the sun, constellations, and the universe. I structured the text in

a way that I thought would seem magical and would capture the wonder of the young boy who explores the starry sky, accompanied by his dog. There are four pages of additional information about the planets and the universe in the back of the book.

Activities

Ask each student to make a constellation with paper stars they have made using yellow or white paper. They can arrange the stars on a black or dark blue sheet of paper. After they have arranged their stars

Stars! Stars! Stars!

Meet the Planets!

The Sun is a medium-size star. All nine of the planets in our solar system orbit the Sun. The Sun has been burning for about 5 billion years.

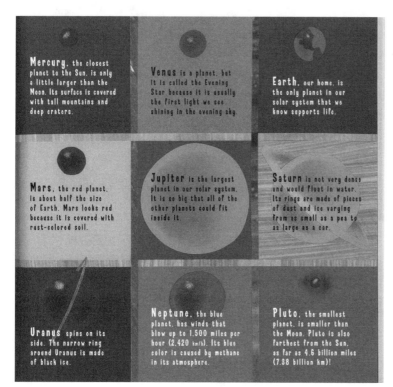

Mercury, the closest planet to the Sun, is only a little larger than the Moon. Its surface is covered with tall mountains and deep craters.

Venus is a planet, but it is called the Evening Star because it is usually the first light we see shining in the evening sky.

Earth, our home, is the only planet in our solar system that we know supports life.

Mars, the red planet, is about half the size of Earth. Mars looks red because it is covered with rust-colored soil.

Jupiter is the largest planet in our solar system. It is so big that all of the other planets could fit inside it.

Saturn is not very dense and would float in water. Its rings are made of pieces of dust and ice varying from as small as a pea to as large as a car.

Uranus spins on its side. The narrow ring around Uranus is made of black ice.

Neptune, the blue planet, has winds that blow up to 1,500 miles per hour (2,420 km/h). Its blue color is caused by methane in its atmosphere.

Pluto, the smallest planet, is smaller than the Moon. Pluto is also farthest from the Sun, as far as 4.6 billion miles (7.38 billion km)!

they can connect them with a line made with a white pencil or crayon, thin strips of paper, or yarn they glue to the surface of the paper. They can make one of the constellations from my book, a constellation they have seen in the night sky, or create a new one as a tribute to their dog, school, or teacher.

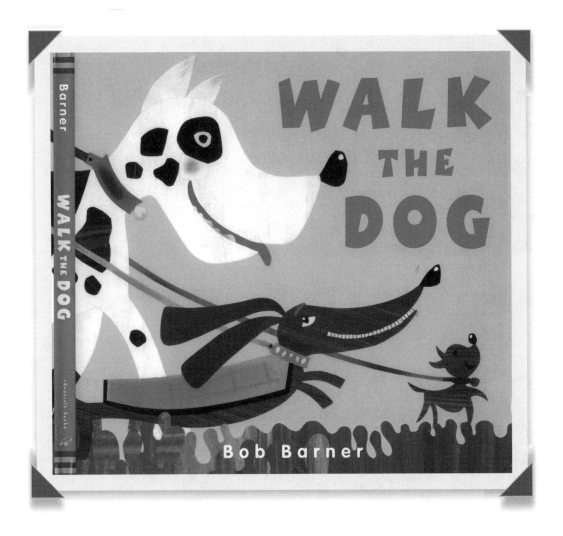

WALK THE DOG

I had the idea for this book while sitting in a coffee shop on the Embarcadero in San Francisco. I never write in public places. I like to sit in my own comfortable studio in my favorite chair and be creative. But on this day I saw something that just seemed like a great

Original Manuscript for *Walk the Dog*

idea. The coffee shop was at a large intersection near the beach. As I drank my coffee I noticed people waiting at the crosswalk to walk their dogs to the park. Then I saw the dogs come off leash and do all of the things dogs like to do in the park—bark, sniff, growl, run, and play, to mention a few. I like my books to work on different levels, much like the layers of a cake. I wanted to have a rather musical

text or chant along with illustrations of the dogs with interesting facts about each dog in the back of the book. Each page begins with the chant "Walk the dog, walk the dog," followed by two words describing what the dog does at the park. "Bark, bark," or "Run, run."

I have found most children to be either musical or at least open to using songs or chants during my presentations. Students are emboldened by the repetition of the chants as the story progresses. It appears to me that the repetition gives them a sense of accomplishment as they work their way through the text. I decided to add another layer of

information by finding a dog for each letter of the alphabet. This worked pretty well, with the exception of a few letters. After much looking, I finally found the only dog in the world that begins with the letter "x": the Xoloitzcuintli, a small Mexican dog with almost no hair. I have a lot of fun spelling the name out rather dramatically and then asking the students to try to pronounce the dog's name. It's very difficult to figure out, so I put a pronunciation guide in the back of the book. Here's how to say Xoloitzcuintli: show-low-eets-QUEEN-tlee. "This is a Mexican dog with almost no hair. Because of its soft warm skin, it was used to warm beds in ancient times." That's a quote about this dog

from the back of the book. There is unique information about all twenty-six dogs in the back of the book. By the end of the presentation everyone in the class seems comfortable and pleased with their pronunciation. I ask the students to try to remember how to say the name and ask their parents for a Xoloitzcuintli when they get home. Then they can definitely say they learned something in school that day that their parents may not know.

I made the paper for the collage art by painting flat white paper sheets with different colors and textures of paint. I painted several sheets in variation for each color. This way I created my own palette of

collage materials to work from. I have had a lot of fun with this book while visiting schools and libraries. Dogs, like dinosaurs, are always popular with kids.

Activities

The students can make an entire pack of dogs in collage using papers in different colors and textures. Each artist can make his or her favorite dog. After the students have signed their work, all of the canines can be assembled on a large sheet of paper or bulletin board.

The teacher can point to the various creations and ask the author of the piece to tell the class a little bit about the breed. Several schools have surprised me with original plays based on my book. Begin by asking the children to choose one of the dogs in the book as their acting part. You can have some students play multiple roles if you have fewer than twenty-six students. The play starts when all of the students chant "Walk the dog, walk the dog." The Airedale, Bulldog, and Chihuahua actors enter stage left saying, "Walk, Walk." This continues in the same form of the book until all twenty-six dogs are on stage. Then they all bark, just like in the book. Each character can then recite the information found in the back of the book about the breed they are portraying. I know this is off, off Broadway, but I love seeing it and the kids certainly have fun with it. Some classes have performed on all fours with optional paper dog-ears they made with construction paper.

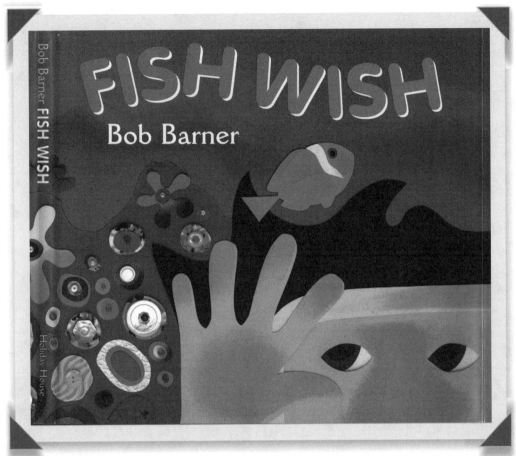

Copyright ©2000 by Bob Barner. Reprinted from *Fish Wish* by permission of Holiday House, Inc.

FISH WISH

Mary Cash, the editor I work with at Holiday House Publishing in New York, asked me to come up with a book about fish. Holiday House didn't have a fish book on their list, and they were looking for an idea. I love to have a request for a title from an editor. I get inspired when I know the editor is actually looking for a specific subject. I thought about all of the kids I had observed at the New England Aquarium when I lived in Boston, looking through the glass tank at the fish. I thought a nice start for the book could be to imagine what life would be like as a fish. *"If I were a fish I would wake up on a coral reef"* starts the first line of the book. I have always loved clownfish, so I decided to make one of them the star of my book. The story gives a lot of

Copyright ©2000 by Bob Barner. Reprinted from *Fish Wish* by permission of Holiday House, Inc.

information about the fish and the other animals that live on the coral reef. The back of the book has facts about the animals in the book as well as the coral reef. I wanted to make the art a magical part of the portal to the new world the boy in the book would discover as he imagined himself as a fish. To do this I used paper collage as well as buttons and beads for the art. Some of the pearl buttons I used to make the coral reef belonged to my wife's great-grandmother.

I had a hard time trying to find or make the paper for the swimsuit for the boy on the last page of the story. I finally found the perfect paper as I was walking through Chinatown in San Francisco one day. I wasn't even thinking about the book, but as soon as I saw that

paper I knew I had to buy it. The paper turned out to be the wrapper for a Chinese candy bar. The candy wasn't great, but the snazzy paper lives on in the last page of *Fish Wish*. I never know where I'll find just the right paper or collage materials when I'm working with collage. That bit of candy wrapper, the antique buttons and beads, have now been seen by thousands of children in both the English and Spanish versions. The printing was so well done on this book that some of the younger readers try to pick up the buttons and beads that appear on the cover. I always get a kick out of their reaction when they discover that the button is only a picture of a button. Kudos to the printer.

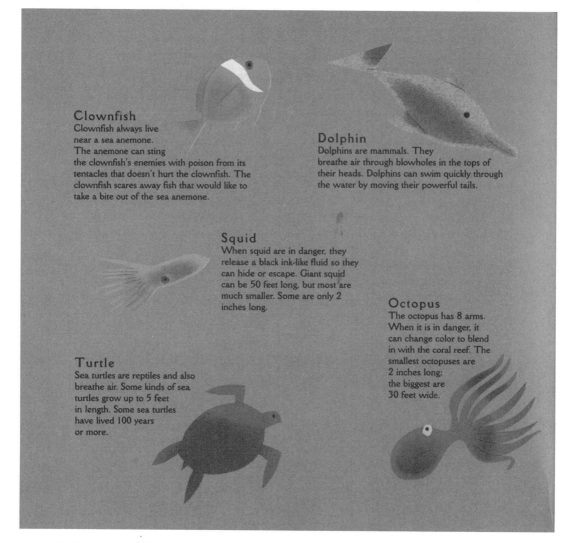

Clownfish
Clownfish always live
near a sea anemone.
The anemone can sting
the clownfish's enemies with poison from its
tentacles that doesn't hurt the clownfish. The
clownfish scares away fish that would like to
take a bite out of the sea anemone.

Dolphin
Dolphins are mammals. They
breathe air through blowholes in the tops of
their heads. Dolphins can swim quickly through
the water by moving their powerful tails.

Squid
When squid are in danger, they
release a black ink-like fluid so they
can hide or escape. Giant squid
can be 50 feet long, but most are
much smaller. Some are only 2
inches long.

Octopus
The octopus has 8 arms.
When it is in danger, it
can change color to blend
in with the coral reef. The
smallest octopuses are
2 inches long;
the biggest are
30 feet wide.

Turtle
Sea turtles are reptiles and also
breathe air. Some kinds of sea
turtles grow up to 5 feet
in length. Some sea turtles
have lived 100 years
or more.

Activities

Start the presentation of this book by asking the students, "Have you ever imagined being an animal? A T-Rex, a polar bear, or a fish?" They will all enthusiastically say yes. Ask them what their day would be like if they were a fish like the one in the book. Talk about the art in the book while you show the cover. Ask the students to look for the little clownfish, who is the star of the book, on every spread as you read the story. Read the story through and then ask what the boy's wish was. Point out that he has put on a bathing suit, mask, and fins so he could swim with a fish just like the one he saw at the aquarium on the first

Hermit Crab
This little crab takes its house with it everywhere it goes! At the first sign of danger the crab pulls its body inside the shell. The largest hermit crabs are 1 foot long.

Shrimp
Some shrimps are as long as 9 inches, but most are much smaller. Shrimps live near the coral reefs in crevices or in burrows they dig in the sand.

Jellyfish
Jellyfish are not fish. They float through the ocean, feeding on tiny plants and animals. Some are less than 1 inch wide; others are wider than 1 foot.

Sea Horse
Sea horses are actually fish. They can be 2–8 inches in size. When sea horses are resting they can use their tiny tails to hold on to seaweed.

Starfish
Starfish are also called sea stars. They are not real fish. Starfish come in many shapes, sizes, and colors. Most starfish have 5 arms, but some have 10 or more.

Sea Anemone
Sea anemones look like flowers, but they are actually animals. They catch small creatures with their stinging tentacles, then stuff them in their mouths. Most sea anemones are 1–2 inches wide, but some are as wide as 3 feet.

page of the book. Show the pages of the book and encourage the class to find all of the animals on each spread. Point out that some of the animals are bigger than the clownfish, and some are smaller. Talk about the collage artwork. Show all of the art in the book created with buttons, beads, and papers. Tell the class that if they choose they may read about the animals in the story and the coral reef on the last pages of the book. If you want to do an art project, you can help each student make a collage picture of his or her favorite fish from the book. Supply construction papers, colorful paper scraps from magazines, buttons, cancelled postage stamps, and any other decorative materials they can stick down with white glue. They can each make a fish on their own

Copyright ©2003 by Bob Barner. Reprinted from *Parade Day* by permission of Holiday House, Inc.

Copyright ©2003 by Bob Barner. Reprinted from *Parade Day* by

colorful sheet of paper, or the fish may be collected and assembled in a school on a larger sheet of paper. Scholastic Publishing produced a wonderful tape using a young boy to read my story and all of the back matter in the book. They also added a beautiful aquatic background sound to the production. At presentations I like to play the tape and watch the students appear enraptured as the young actor does a great job reading my story.

PARADE DAY

I love a good parade. I didn't know of any children's books on the subject and started to do some research about parades both well known and obscure. I wanted to layer the parade text with the idea of a parade for each month of the year and introduce the calendar to K–1 students. This is another concept book—an introduction to the calendar. This is a very important part of the daily orientation teachers present to their kindergarten students. The teacher will present the day of the week, the month of the year, the date, and the calendar year. Some teachers will recite the number of the day in the year and how many days remain in the calendar year. Two excellent events, Easter and Chinese

permission of Holiday House, Inc.

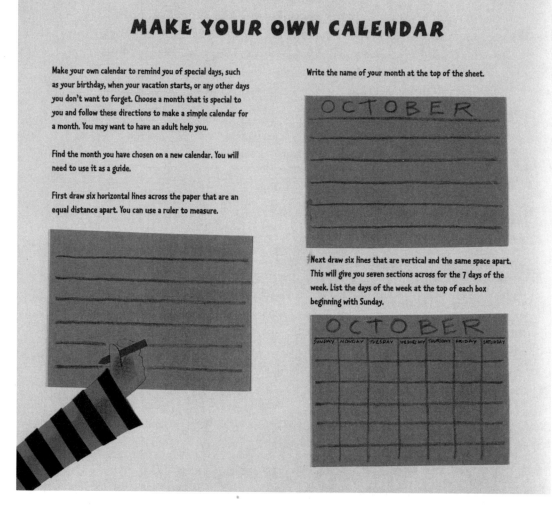

MAKE YOUR OWN CALENDAR

Make your own calendar to remind you of special days, such as your birthday, when your vacation starts, or any other days you don't want to forget. Choose a month that is special to you and follow these directions to make a simple calendar for a month. You may want to have an adult help you.

Find the month you have chosen on a new calendar. You will need to use it as a guide.

First draw six horizontal lines across the paper that are an equal distance apart. You can use a ruler to measure.

Write the name of your month at the top of the sheet.

Next draw six lines that are vertical and the same space apart. This will give you seven sections across for the 7 days of the week. List the days of the week at the top of each box beginning with Sunday.

Copyright ©2003 by Bob Barner. Reprinted from *Parade Day* by permission of Holiday House, Inc.

New Year, don't always occur in the same month year to year. I was sorry to lose these illustrative parades, but I thought it best to choose parades that occurred in the same month every year to avoid confusion with the youngest readers. The art was a challenge for this book. I thought a long line of parading people on every page could make the art monotonous. As I sketched the layouts for each page I tried to think of different perspectives or viewpoints for each picture. I like to put personal references in some of the illustrations in my books when possible. On the Halloween parade page I added dinosaur, bug, fish, and skeleton costumes—thinly veiled references to some of my earlier books.

Check the calendar you are using as a guide to see which day begins the month. Number the days starting with the number 1 and ending with 28, 29, 30, or 31.

Put your calendar on the wall or on the refrigerator with a magnet. Check it every day to see when your next special day is coming up. You can make calendars for the other 11 months and have a calendar for the whole year.

Color in your special days with markers or colored pencil, or decorate them with stickers, rubber stampings, glitter, or drawings. Print your special information in the blocks. Every day that passes can be crossed off with a mark, so you can keep track of your month.

Activities

Parade Day is all about parades and using the calendar. After reading the rhyming text to the class, go back through the book and ask the children to say the name of each month as you turn the pages. Point out the collage illustrations. Lead the students in a collage and calendar-making workshop. Follow the directions for calendar-making on pages 30 and 31. Each student may want to make a calendar of his or her birthday or another special time.

Copyright ©2004 by Bob Barner. Reprinted from *Bug Safari* by permission of Holiday House, Inc.

BUG SAFARI

With this book I wanted to accomplish three goals: write a book with more text than I usually use in my books, write a book for slightly older readers, and let the art style evolve to the next level. I came up with the idea of a young explorer on a safari finding himself lost in the jungle and deciding to follow a long line of ants in hopes of getting back to civilization. I was inspired by some of the old *Tarzan* safari movies I watched as a kid. I wanted to capture some of the safari expedition's sense of danger and adventure in my book. I enjoyed writing a story without rhyme and having the freedom to use more text to create a mood. With the art I decided to use thick painted lines on some of the shapes. My wife and I made much of the collage paper used in the book at a paste paper class. We made papers with a flour or sugar paint concoction. Paste papers are decorated by combing through the wet surface with different patterns and textures. When I picked up the dried papers the next day I was surprised with the result. Each piece was more beautiful than the other. It was only then that I thought of using the papers to make the book more unique. These were paper designs that weren't for sale at any art supply store. I used a large paint-brush loaded with black paint to define some of the shapes in the art. The black lines give the art a very bold look and helped the bright colors pop off the page.

After I did the pencil sketches for each page, I chose a selection of papers for the palette on each page. I usually like to start with the large objects or background and work my way up to the foreground and the small details. I cut out all of the pieces and move them around or change pieces until I like the overall feeling. One of my favorite things about this book is how the giant boy is usually hidden by plants while he examines the bugs he encounters on the safari. On a few of the pages he is hard to see at first. This is exactly the effect I wanted to achieve. The back of the book has information about the bugs in the book. I find this format very useful to the way I like to structure the books. I like to include information throughout the book while being careful not to weigh down the text with facts that I may find difficult to incorporate into the story. With this design the teacher can read the book and then refer to the factual information in the back of the book. Having read the story text and been presented with the illustrations, reviewing the facts at the back of the book will be of more interest to the students. They will associate the information with the story they have just heard and with the collage art they have seen.

Activities

After reading the story to the children, ask them who they think are the real stars of the book. I hope they'll choose the red and black ants. Ask them to remember and list the types of other bugs that also appear in the book. The boy in the book studies the insects and makes notes and drawings in his notebook. Show the pages where the boy is studying or measuring the ants or other bugs in the book. The class members can each make a notebook with drawings and information about the bugs in the story. They can also add some favorite bugs

I was lost in a bug-infested jungle one hot summer day. I was all alone, looking for a way back to base camp, when I saw a long line of marching black ants. Where could they be going? It looked like an ant safari. Was this a way out of the jungle? I decided to follow.

Bugs in the Book

Most of the creatures in this book are insects. An insect has three body parts: a head, an abdomen, and a thorax. These three parts are easy to see in an ant but harder to see in insects such as ladybugs or walking sticks. All insects also have six legs.

Bug is a word used to describe many small creatures. See if you can guess which two bugs on this page are not insects.

Stag Beetle Only the male stag beetle has big jaws. The beetles use their big jaws in fights. The female lays its eggs in decaying wood, and the larvae eat it after hatching.

Cricket Field crickets are common all over North America. Crickets make a musical sound by rubbing their forewings together.

Dung Beetle A dung beetle, or tumblebug, lays one egg in a ball of dung it has collected. Then it buries the ball in the ground. When the larva hatches, it eats the dung.

Centipedes are arthropods, not insects. Arthropods have bodies with many sections and two legs on each section. Most centipedes are active at night and hide under stones or leaves during the day.

Bug Safari by permission of Holiday House, Inc.

Bug Safari by permission of Holiday House, Inc.

that are not in the book. Assemble a collection of collage papers and let the students make a collage of their favorite bug. Be sure to ask them to sign their name on the art when they are done. This book can inspire activities about bugs as well as simple mapping skills. Have half of the class make a red ant out of paper. Have the other half make a black collage ant. On a large sheet of paper, a bulletin board, or a blank wall, tape the ant parade in a long undulating line. The artists will see their ant on its way to a picnic, a piece of cake, or perhaps to their own school.

Copyright ©2005 by Bob Barner. Reprinted from *Where Crocodiles Have Wings* by permission of Holiday House, Inc.

WHERE CROCODILES HAVE WINGS

Regina Griffin, senior editor at Holiday House in New York, asked me to take a look at a manuscript she thought I might enjoy illustrating. I usually don't illustrate books written by other people. I seem to keep busy trying to do the illustrations for the work I create myself. When I read Patricia McKissack's manuscript about flying crocodiles, I fell in love with the story immediately. I imagined all of the fun I could have designing the fantastic characters she had created for this wonderful story. I wanted to continue with the art technique I used for *Bug Safari*. I did the sketches for the pages with a very large black marker. The wide-tipped marker forced me to draw in a very loose and stylized way. I chose the collage papers that I thought would bring together

Holiday House / New York

patterns and colors in an unexpected way. I felt that this visual treatment would complement the wonderful, fanciful text.

This was the first book I worked on in my new studio since our move to Green Street. I was happy to have all of the moving boxes unpacked and to be back to work. I relished the simple pleasure of having the time to be creative and doing what I love to do. I had been collecting papers made by students and given to me at schools I had visited on author day. The papers were filled with fantastic colors and textures. It's amazing how uninhibited and creative young artists can be. I wanted to use some of the beautiful patterns they had created in my collage work. The result was very satisfying and possibly

Have Wings by permission of Holiday House, Inc.

one of the best graphic assemblages I have ever done. I felt energized with the students' papers and thought that the collaboration was quite appropriate since the end user would again be young students. It was a very nice moment when I heard from the editor that the arrival of my box of brightly colored art had made her day. Everyone likes to be appreciated.

Activities

My collage art evolved a bit more with the making of this book. I used papers from all kinds of sources. Gift wrap, fancy paper bags, and

Copyright ©2005 by Bob Barner. Reprinted from *Where Crocodiles*

papers I printed myself were used, as well as colored sheets from the art store. After reading the book to the students for the first time, go through the pages again and ask them to identify each animal and to count all of the different papers used in each piece of art. You can then ask the students to collect papers, feathers, buttons, beads, bags decorated with patterns, and any other graphic material from home. The next day they can create a large resource table filled with all of the unused and wonderful raw materials they will use to create their own versions of the animals in my book or another animal that is a favorite. This little exercise will help the students see that art can be made

Have Wings by permission of Holiday House, Inc.

from almost anything and that sharing their found treasures can be lots of fun.

Patricia McKissack uses rhymes to tell the story in *Where Crocodiles Have Wings*. Older students may enjoy a writing project in addition to the collage session. Ask the students to create a world as a series of situations with rhyming text that present a unique and delightful new world, much as Patricia McKissack has done in this book. Ask the students to study and comment on the different activities happening in the book. Ask them to describe what was done in the text and the pictures to help create a funny and special time and place. Younger readers may enjoy talking about a favorite bedtime book that they like to read before they go to sleep. Very young readers may like sharing their favorite bedtime book and animals from home on show-and-tell day. Invite them to create some collage art using their own stuffed animals and books for inspiration.

A Day in the Life of an Artist

GETTING STARTED IN THE MORNING

I work in a studio in my home. I'm lucky to have a view of the Golden Gate Bridge and the Pacific Ocean out one of the windows. I know a lot of very smart people who say they would spend the whole day watching TV or standing in front of the refrigerator if they worked at home. I know they're kidding, but I've never had a problem sticking to business. I like to start my work day with a strong cup of coffee and the newspaper in my office. I have a habit of making a list of things I want to accomplish the next day at the end of each day. The list is the first thing I look at while I have my morning coffee or two. Some days are broken up with many different tasks like sketching, writing, answering e-mail, or mailing packages of art, while others are spent working on a single page of a book I'm illustrating. I try to make each day a little different than the one before. This helps me keep things fresh.

The design of my studio is very important to me. I can't concentrate if there is clutter and chaos. I have tried to design a tranquil and peaceful place where my imagination will be inspired to create the stories and illustrations for my books. I have had many studio spaces during my career. Some of them have been small and cramped, while others were spacious and airy. Interestingly, it doesn't really seem to matter what size or shape a studio space is as long as I feel organized in the room. I like to have a long, flat table to work on. Since most of my work is done in collage, a traditional slanted designer's table doesn't work for me. All of my papers slide off the table onto the floor. I use a good quality task light, a taboret to hold supplies, some filing cabinets, and a good chair, nothing too exotic or exciting. Several people have asked me where I work while standing in the middle of my studio. Some people have a romantic notion that an artist's studio should be filled with easels holding works in progress, huge stacks of paper, and many empty wine bottles. My space is usually fairly neat so that I can find my supplies and papers and get my work done.

I've tried being messy, but I just spend a lot of time trying to locate things in the chaos. My first studio was in Boston. I had a neat little alcove just off the bedroom. I set up a table and worked there very happily for the first five years of my career. My Airedale terrier, Bo, kept me company all day. He watched me work until the wee hours of every morning as I watched him sleep luxuriously on the floor next to me. I had my photograph taken with Bo for the back of my first book, *The Elephant's Visit*. He was a great pal and my first roommate. When I got married we moved to a much larger apartment and I had my own room to use as a studio for the first time. It was a great treat to have the luxury of space. My favorite part of having the separate studio space was that I could close the door when things got really messy in the middle of a collage project. After a few days of working on a collage for a book, I have hundreds of little paper bits on the floor. The studio had a window seat that overlooked Mt. Vernon Street on Beacon Hill. My constant companion while I worked was my wife's dog, Ludwig. Luddie was a curious little character who loved to spend his days looking out the window from his second floor perch. I guess he was my longest-standing employee. Everything went just fine until he broke into hysterical barking if a dog he didn't like walked under our window. These surprise bark attacks caused more than a few slips of the pen and quite a few do-overs for me. We also had a little house in Duxbury, Massachusetts, just south of Boston. I had a wonderful white, sunny work space on the second floor of that house. That's where I did the art for *Benny's Pennies* and a few of the *Start Smart Math* books for Doubleday as well.

Today I work in my San Francisco studio. It's a simple space with great light, and it's very close to some great coffee shops and restaurants. For the past three years I have been lucky to rent a little house in Sonoma, California, for the summer. Having outside space in that beautiful inspiring scenery adds a whole new dimension to the kind of work I want to do. It's great to go outside and be messy with watercolors, pastel, graphite, or whatever materials I want to experiment with. I have spent many happy hours under the gazebo working with all sorts of media while looking down the hill to the groomed rows of grapevines. I like to use my time there to try new techniques. An interesting thing happens when you work in a beautiful place like Sonoma. It seems impossible to have a bad idea or make a bad piece of art. Of course this isn't true, but the atmosphere is so nurturing that I seem to feel good about almost everything I do. Since my wife has a nine-to-five job, I try to keep civilized working hours. I usually start my workday when my wife leaves in the morning at about eight o'clock. I try to end my work when she comes home in the evening at about seven. Since I don't have many meetings and I have no commute time, I really do get quite a bit done in a day.

ART, PHONE CALLS, AND WRITING

I seem to have four jobs: writing and illustrating books, illustration, speaking at schools and conferences, and selling my original art. I have to juggle all of these tasks every day and still meet the deadlines for the books I want to publish. Help! It's a constant struggle to keep everything in balance. When I have a tight book deadline I simply have to let everything else but the art I'm doing for the book wait. I am very focused when I'm creating the art for a book. I actually enjoy the single-mindedness and the periods of extreme focus and effort.

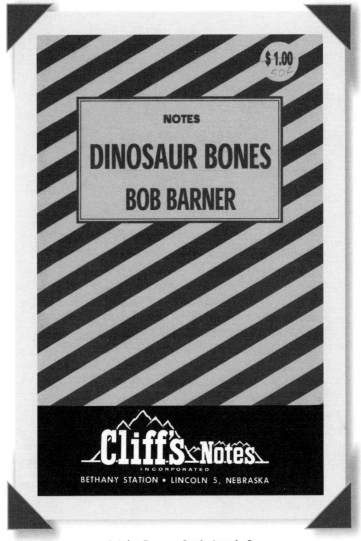

A Joke From a Guy's Lunch Guy

GUY'S LUNCH

Working alone can get a bit tedious at times. There usually aren't any of the typical interruptions that happen in an office setting. I've developed the ability over the years to stick with whatever I'm working on for a very long time. I try to remind myself to take a walk, go get a coffee, or have lunch with some of my colleagues when I can. There has been an institution in San Francisco for the past twenty-five years or so, Guy's Lunch. A core group of guys—writers, artists, photographers, and designers—has been meeting for lunch six days a week at

restaurants in Chinatown and North Beach. It's great to get away from my drawing table and compare notes with other creative types from time to time. I always feel inspired and ready to work when I come back to the studio.

MANAGING THE BUSINESS: SCHOOL VISITS, BOOK SIGNINGS, CONTRACTS, AND DEADLINES

I spend much of my day juggling several tasks that I have to complete to keep my business going. Rarely do I have the luxury to just do one thing like draw or write. My work life changes from time to time as well. After the publication of a new book, I usually have a number of signings at bookstores as well as conferences to attend. This is a good way to get the book in the stores and in front of the public. During the school year I like to do a number of school visits, usually twenty to forty each year. Many schools have a visiting author program that provides funds and planning for one or as many as four authors each school year. The author visits may also be funded by a PTO or a grant. It's always nice to get back home from a road trip or just a day at a school. The time I spend in schools is very rewarding. I get new ideas for presentations, books, and other projects. When I'm back in the studio after an author visit I seem to get all fired up and excited about what I do all over again. Many of the images in my books are licensed for use by card companies or for foreign rights to publish my books in other countries. My literary agent, Liza Voges, usually takes care of these arrangements for me. My original collage art is sold through galleries or directly to clients when someone contacts me about a piece they admire.

Author/Illustrator Visit

An author visit can be one of the most important experiences a young student can have. A chance to hear the author talk about his or her work can motivate and encourage readers, writers, or budding artists to approach their interests with new enthusiasm. After you have chosen an author to visit your school or library, it's most important to prepare the students for the experience. The preparation should begin weeks before the author arrives. Stu-

dents should be introduced to the author's books and share art and writing activities. Classes may be coached in an author study to know a little about the life and work of the person they will be meeting. Groundwork done before the visit will ultimately make the author day more enjoyable and memorable for teachers and students. To familiarize the students with the author, a set of the author's books should be on display in the library when the approaching visit is announced. In the library or classrooms, a selection of the books should be read with the students and discussed. The art in the books should be displayed and the techniques used to create it should be shared with all of the young artists. I love to see the wonderful collage projects that hang on the walls when I visit a school. The kids seem to like working with papers, and they always surprise me with their creativity. While discussing the books with students, I think it's important to explore the different levels of each book. I like to include art, music, rhyming text, and facts in many of my nonfiction books. If we take the time to celebrate books and the people who create them with students, we have a chance of developing a new generation of readers who like to read and write and who love books.

A BOB BARNER AUTHOR/ILLUSTRATOR VISIT

Author day is a special day for the students, the teachers and volunteers, and for me—the author. It's great to get out of my studio and

actually meet the people who like to read my books. I like to make every presentation different, depending on class grade level and the size of the group. I've done hundreds of presentations over the years. I have been invited to Massachusetts, New York, New Hampshire, Pennsylvania, Florida, North Carolina, South Carolina, Georgia, Alabama, Tennessee, Washington, California, Mexico, and Guam. I think I turned a corner with my presentations when I visited the island of Guam in 1999. The Guam Council of the International Reading Association asked me to come to their annual meeting and visit schools for one week. Shortly after deplaning I was speaking to about 500 teachers. Over the next week it seems I spoke to just about every class on the island. The temperature was 104 the day I landed. The weather did

cool off later in the week, but it was very hot all the time I was there. The teachers I met were dedicated, enthusiastic, and very involved with their students. I visited several schools and did presentations to classrooms and to assemblies in libraries and gymnasiums.

The last two days I presented at the old naval theatre. I saw 500 students at a time in a very large venue with no air conditioning. It was very hot, and I was afraid the kids would wiggle through the entire forty-five-minute assembly. I think the turning point came when I was faced with this challenge. I just decided to have a good time and go with the flow. I played some music, drew some pictures, read some books, and even answered questions. I made six presentations in that theatre during two days. The kids were all fantastic audiences. They laughed at every joke, applauded at the end of every drawing, and asked great questions. We all had a wonderful time in spite of the heat and the cavernous size of the room. After my wonderful trial by fire in Guam, I have become fearless of large crowds or adverse conditions.

Having said that, I must admit that I feel more confident when I like the room in which I'll be presenting. It's important to find out what your visiting author needs to make the visit the best it can be. One of my other favorite school visit experiences has been with my friend Joan Stevenson in South Carolina. Joan is a retired teacher who thinks that seeing a visiting author in school is one of the most enriching experiences a child can have. Joan likes to book me for a week of school visits at a time. She picks me up at the airport in her white van filled with my books. By the end of the week I have spoken to 2,000 or more children, and most of the book boxes are empty. Because Joan and the schools do such a great job of preparation for the presentations before I arrive, it's a wonderful experience for me and for the students I speak to. I start my presentations with a brief introduction of myself and let the audience know what I'll be doing during the forty-five-minute assembly. I like to kick things off by playing a CD of the song "Dem Bones" as I draw the bones in time to the music. I bring along lots of show-and-tell to help explain all of the steps in the book-making process.

I show original sketches, large blowups of my art, the mockup dummy of a book, and comment notes from editors. I read some of the books or talk about some of the things that happened while I was working on them. I show my little idea book and talk about how I get ideas and how I do research. My goal is to entertain the students while sharing with them some of the experiences I've had while making books. At the end of the presentation, I want the students to be excited about reading, writing, or making their own books. One of my favorite things is to get a note from a teacher who tells me that the students are still talking about the day that Bob Barner came to school last year.

At the end of each session, if we have time, children like to ask questions. Some of the most frequently asked questions involve questions about what I like, my writing, and what pets I have.

Questions Frequently Asked by Kids

Q. Could you always draw?

A. No. I had to practice a lot. I was fortunate to have great art teachers. I majored in art at college for four years and practiced my drawing every day.

Q. How do you get ideas for books?

A. I get ideas by looking at nature, reading books, or watching a nature show on TV.

Q. Do you ever make mistakes?

A. I make mistakes almost every day. If I have a hard time drawing something, I try to find a picture of it in the library or on the Internet.

Q. Do you have a dog?

A. No.

Q. What's your favorite color?

A. Blue.

Q. Do you have a hobby?

A. Yes. I like to play the guitar. I started playing when I was eight years old.

Q. Is your mustache real?

A. Yes.

Q. When did you start drawing?

A. I'm told I started drawing at the age of three.

Q. What books did you read as a kid?

A. I read library books and Golden Books my parents bought at the supermarket. I had *Jack and the Beanstalk*, *Pinocchio*, and lots of dinosaur books.

Q. How do you get the words and art you draw into the book?

A. All of the art that I make for the books is photographed.

The images from the camera are put into a computer. A book designer puts the words in the computer, together with the pictures (images).

If you have more questions, you may find the answers on my Web site. Visit http://www.bobbarner.com for more information.

Dem Bones, The Movie

In 2004 I was thrilled when Weston Woods Studios asked permission to make a film from my book *Dem Bones*. Weston Woods was celebrating its fiftieth year, and I knew them for making wonderful films with the best of picture books. The project was done with the help of a company called Zippitoons based in Wellington, New Zealand. Zippitoons and Weston Woods shared the storyboards with me as the process moved along. Gary McGivney of Zippitoons, Melissa Reilly, and Paul Gagne of Weston Woods managed to bring my paper skeletons to life. Actually, I know they used a lot of very talented computer graphics technicians, designers, and filmmakers.

An original version of the 200-year-old "Dem Bones" song was recorded to accompany the film. Raul Malo and his New Orleans jazz band played a humorous and spirited rendition of the song to accompany my dancing skeletons. When the video arrived, I popped it in the VCR right away. I watched the eight-minute film three times before I could think of anything to say. It's as if the images really did just jump off the pages and start dancing around. I was astounded and very happy with the results. Every word I had written in the back matter was included in the film. I've had a chance to view the film with several K–3 audiences. The filmmakers have done a fabulous job of making the information in the book very accessible to an even wider audience than the book.

- *"Bob Barner's book is brought to bone-shaking life in this animated musical that connects song to information. Raul Malo's toe-tapping music makes this skeleton band rattle and tickles the funny bone."*
  - **2004 ALA Notable Video Committee**
  - **Best of the Best List, Heart of Texas Literature Center**
  - **Worldfest-Houston, Silver Remi**

I SEE STARS!

In 2005 Weston Woods honored me by making a wonderful film based on my book *Stars! Stars! Stars!* The animation was done by Zippi-toons, the New Zealand-based film company that did the work on the *Dem Bones* film. The finished video looks magical to me, and the spacey music is truly out of this world. All of the information that I included in the book is made even more interesting and is more easily under-stood with the movement of the animation and the very evocative sound track.

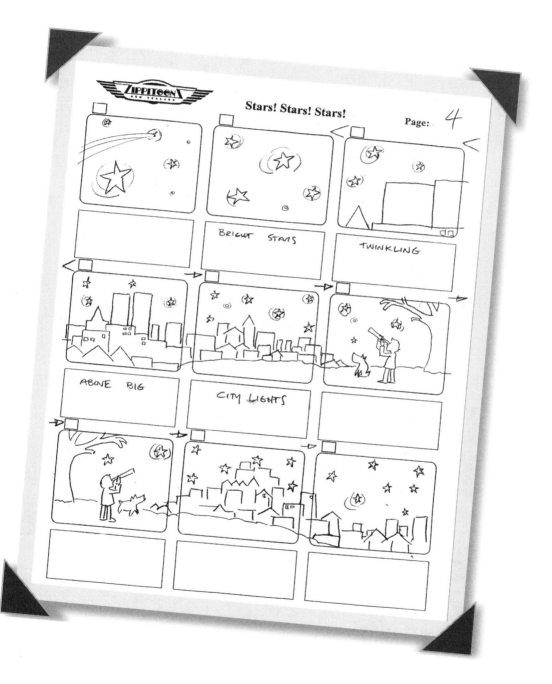

DINOSAURS!

In 2006, Weston Woods decided to create a film based on this book. The animation was done by Zippitoons, the New Zealand-based film company that did the work on the two previous films.

Appendix A: Bibliography

BOOKS WRITTEN AND ILLUSTRATED BY BOB BARNER

The Elephant's Visit. Boston: Atlantic-Little, Brown, 1975.
Elephant Facts. New York: E. P. Dutton, 1979.
The Elevator Escalator Book. New York: Doubleday, 1990.
Space Race. New York: Bantam Doubleday Dell, 1995.
How to Weigh an Elephant. New York: Bantam Doubleday Dell, 1995.
Dinosaurs Depart. New York: Bantam Doubleday Dell, 1996.
Too Many Dinosaurs. New York: Bantam Doubleday Dell, 1995.
Dem Bones. San Francisco: Chronicle Books, 1996.
To Everything. San Francisco: Chronicle Books, 1998.
Which Way to the Revolution? New York: Holiday House, 1998.
Bugs! Bugs! Bugs! San Francisco: Chronicle Books, 1999.
Walk the Dog. San Francisco: Chronicle Books, 2000.
Fish Wish. New York: Holiday House, 2000.
Dinosaur Bones. San Francisco: Chronicle Books, 2001.
Stars! Stars! Stars! San Francisco: Chronicle Books, 2002.
Parade Day. New York: Holiday House, 2003.
Bug Safari. New York: Holiday House, 2005.
Penguin Party. San Francisco: Chronicle Books, 2007
Dinosaur Wings. San Francisco: Chronicle Books, 2007
Sleepy Snow. San Francisco: Chronicle Books, 2008

BOOKS ILLUSTRATED BY BOB BARNER

Aarle, Van. *Don't Put Your Cart Before the Horse Race.* Boston: Houghton Mifflin, 1980.
Bernstein, Joann E., and Paul Cohen. *Riddles to Take on Vacation.* Niles, Ill.: Albert Whitman and Company, 1980.
Brisson, Pat. *Benny's Pennies.* New York: Doubleday, 1993.
Bunting, Eve. *We Need a Bigger Zoo.* Boston: Ginn and Company, 1974.
Demuth, Patricia Brennan. *Pick Up Your Ears, Henry.* New York: Macmillan, 1992.
Lewis, J. Patrick. *Big is Big and Little Little.* New York: Holiday House, 2007
McKissack, Patricia. *Where Crocodiles Have Wings.* New York: Holiday House, 2006.
Segaloff, Nat, and Paul Erickson. *Fish Tales.* New York: Sterling, 1990.
Todd, Traci N. *Wiggle, Waggle, Loop-de-Loo!* Greensboro, N.C.: Kindermusic, 2003.
Wolcott, Patty. *Double-Decker, Double-Decker, Double-Decker Bus.* Boston: Addison-Wesley, 1980.

VIDEOS

A Dog's Dream. Boston: Allyn and Bacon, 1979.
Mass Performances. Cambridge: Massachusetts Corporation for Educational TV, 1994.
Dem Bones. Norwalk, Conn.: Weston Woods, 2003.
Stars! Stars! Stars! Norwalk, Conn.: Weston Woods, 2005.
Dinosaur Bones. Norwalk, Conn.: Weston Woods, 2006

EDUCATIONAL PUBLISHING

Mrs. Seal's Fish Chowder. Boston: Houghton Mifflin, 1977.
Mr. Elephant's Park. Boston: Houghton Mifflin, 1977.
The Bike Race. Boston: Houghton Mifflin, 1991.
The Good Friends Club. Boston: Houghton Mifflin, 1991.

Appendix B: Author Interview

CLA Briefings—Author Interview

Interview reprinted from the California Library Association Newsletter, conducted by Penny Peck, Senior Librarian Youth Services, San Leandro Public Library.

Penny Peck: Many of your picture books are nonfiction books, like *Dem Bones* (Chronicle Books, 1996) or *Stars! Stars! Stars!* (Chronicle Books, 2002). Do you have a special interest in science or history?

> **Bob Barner:** I have a keen interest in science, art, and music. I try to put all three of these to use in my books when I can. It worked out well with *Dem Bones*.

PP: Any new books coming out this spring or fall you can tell us about?

> **BB:** Yes! *Where Crocodiles Have Wings*, Holiday House, comes out this fall. [Editor's note: fall of 2005] I did the illustrations for Patricia McKissack's story. It's a wonderful bedtime book with fantastic images that I had a great time illustrating. I'm very pleased to be a part of the project.

PP: Do you usually write the text of your books as well as doing the illustrations, or do you often illustrate books that others have written the text for?

> **BB:** I usually write and illustrate my own books. If something exceptional comes along, like the McKissack book, I will do the illustrations.

PP: Was your first book *Benny's Pennies*? (It's a personal favorite of mine because of my name.) How did you get your foot in the door of the publishing industry?

> **BB:** Well, I've been asked to be part of *The Author and You* series being published by Libraries Unlimited. I've been trying to remember all sorts of details for that book. *The Elephant's Visit* (Little, Brown, 1975) was my first book. *Benny's Pennies*, by Pat Brisson (Doubleday), was published in 1993.
>
> I got my foot in the door by knocking on many of them. When I graduated from art school I moved to Boston, Massachusetts, from Columbus, Ohio, to work in publishing. It was difficult, but I had energy and youth on my side. I was fortunate to meet a lot of editors who liked my work and helped me get a start.

PP: Are most of your illustrations done in collage? Or other techniques?

> **BB:** Collage is my technique of choice now. I like the way it reproduces in the books.

PP: Is there any artist who inspired you? Or other picture book illustrators you always look forward to seeing new work from?

> **BB:** I love James Marshall's books. I look forward to seeing Lois Elhert's books.

PP: Do you visit schools and public libraries to talk to kids about your books?

BB: Yes. I love to get out of the studio and meet the people who use the books.

PP: If so, how can librarians contact you for visits?

BB: Just write to me at: bobbarner@aol.com, or visit www.bobbarner.com

PP: How many schools or libraries do you visit each month (or year)?

BB: I visit twenty to forty each school year.

PP: I saw a photo on your Web site of you holding a guitar at a school visit. Do you play and/or sing with the students?

BB: Yes. I draw a skeleton while we listen to a nice recording of the "Dem Bones" song, read some of my books, show sketches and blowups of my art, and talk about making a book. If the students will sing along, we all sing "Dem Bones" together. I leave some time for questions and answers. I started playing the guitar when I was eight years old.

PP: Any funny experiences at a school or library visit? Nearly every author or illustrator has a story about the visit that went awry!

BB: Yes. Big time in South Carolina. The fire marshal decided to have fire drills the day I was at the school doing presentations. It was awful. The lights went out and sirens sounded. The kids did a great job filing out and left me on the stage holding a microphone. The fire department did this during all three presentations. Yikes!

PP: When you were a kid, did you have a favorite book? Did you go to the library very often?

BB: I had many favorite books and I did go to the library often, especially the town library in Eastlake, Ohio, where I grew up. I loved picture books about dinosaurs, outer space, and animals. Later on I liked Jules Verne and H. G. Wells.

PP: You now live in San Francisco but are from Arkansas. What inspired you to live in California? Is your wife from here?

BB: I was born in Arkansas, but we moved to Ohio when I was a few weeks old. I went to college in Columbus, Ohio, and then moved to Boston, Massachusetts. After twenty years, my wife and I moved to San Francisco. We like the creative community and the culture here. And the lack of snow.

PP: Any thoughts on the current state of libraries in California?

BB: I'm very distressed with the state of library funding. I was happy to see that a disaster was diverted in Salinas recently. Music, art, and libraries played a very important part of my development as a child. I think about it every day. I think we will all need to be creative to keep this wonderful resource available for our young people.

PP: Anything else you would like our readers to know?

BB: I would like to thank all of the librarians for the fine job they are doing. I wish all of you luck, and I hope we have a chance to meet in the future.

Index

About the Author

BOB BARNER is the author and illustrator of several award winning non-fiction picture books for children including *Dem Bones, Stars! Stars! Stars!* and *Bugs! Bugs! Bugs!* He resides in San Francisco, California, and maintains the Web site www.bobbarner.com.